Oh, Grow Up!

The Everyday Miracle
of Becoming More Like Jesus

by Tom Kraeuter

Emerald Books

P.O. Box 635
Lynnwood, WA 98046

TRAINING RESOURCES
8929 Old LeMay Ferry Rd.
Hillsboro MO 63050

Oh, Grow Up!
The Everyday Miracle of Becoming More Like Jesus
© 2001 Training Resources, Inc.
8929 Old LeMay Ferry Road
Hillsboro, MO 63050
(636) 789-4522
www.training-resources.org

Published by Emerald Books
P.O. Box 635
Lynnwood, WA 98046

ISBN 1-883002-88-5

Printed in the United States of America.

DEDICATION

I humbly dedicate this book to
my dear friends Philip and Mary Mahder.

Phil and Mary, your friendship has blessed me.
Your willingness to always follow God
has inspired me.
Your consistent display of the principles
in this book has amazed me.
Thank you for being examples,
fellow sojourners, and special friends.
I love you!

THANKS TO...

The congregation of Christian Outreach Church for so often demonstrating the principles I am sharing in this book. Your caring and love have frequently overwhelmed me.

Jennifer Brody, my editor. Your involvement at an earlier stage than usual caused this to become a much better book than it otherwise might have been. Thanks so much for challenging me, helping me, and making me sound like a better writer than I am.

Those who reviewed the manuscript prior to publication and offered lots of helpful suggestions, including:
- Pastor Randall Burns, Military Street Baptist Church, Houlton, Maine
- Pastor Nick Ittzes, Christian Outreach Church, Hillsboro, Missouri
- Pastor David Johnson, Amery Free Lutheran Church, Amery, Wisconsin
- Pastor Alan Kraft, Christ Community Evangelical Free Church, Greeley, Colorado
- Laurie Mellinger, Lancaster, Pennsylvania, who challenged my thinking a lot!

Special thanks to my wife and family for constant encouragement, faithful support, and undying loyalty. Barb, David, Stephen, and Amy, you're the best!

CONTENTS

What Is Our Part in Developing Character?

How Else Does God Build Character Into Us?

CHAPTER 1

BECOMING MORE LIKE JESUS

S ome time ago I saw two children playing together. As they played, one of them was being selfish with the toys. The other responded in a very matter-of-fact way, "Oh, grow up!" He was not saying it in a mean or derogatory way. His statement was not an attempt to belittle his friend. The child simply wanted his companion to act like he knew he should. The friend was acting immaturely even though he obviously knew better.

I immediately realized that the church in America needs that same type of advice. We already know far more than we live. We have more seminars and conferences, advances and retreats, and books and tapes than anywhere else in the world. However, despite this deluge of teaching, we seem to be producing the weakest form of Christianity on earth.

Jesus summarized His Sermon on the Mount by stating that a person who hears His words and puts them into practice will be like a man who built his house on a rock. With such a solid foundation, that person won't need to be concerned about his life falling apart during the storms of life. But simply hearing the words, according to Jesus, is not enough. They must be put into practice.

> *He replied simply, "She translated the Bible every single day...into life."*

I recently heard a story about an agricultural agent visiting a farmer. The agent wanted the farmer to attend a meeting that would help him become a better farmer. No matter what the agent said, the farmer simply refused to come. Finally, exasperated, the agent asked the farmer why he didn't want to learn how to do his job better. The farmer replied, "I'm only farming half as well as I know how right now. Why would I want to learn more before I put into practice what I already know?"

Hmmm. That kind of reminds me of James' exhortation to us: "Do not merely listen to the word, and so deceive yourselves. Do what it says" (James 1:22). We need to put into practice the things we already know from God's word.

One day a group of seminary students asked their theology professor which translation of the Bible he preferred—the KJV or NIV or NASB or NKJV, or which? After thinking for a moment, he answered, "I prefer my mother's translation." The students were bewildered. "Which translation," they asked, "was your mother a part of?" He replied simply, "She translated the Bible every single day...into life."

As Christians we can say all of the right and proper words, but if those words are not reflected in our lives, are they really of much value? People will always learn far more from our actions than they do from our words. The fact is that we are the only Bibles that many people in the world will ever read. What are they reading in our lives? The things we do, the way we live, should simply be an extension of our faith in and confession of Jesus Christ as our Savior.

I have too often heard Christians offer an excuse for acting badly in a particular situation. "It's just my personality. It's the way I am." That may be true, but it does not excuse sin. Your personality—your character—needs to change.

Our goal as Christians is Christ-likeness: to become more like Jesus each and every day. Romans 8:29 tells us, "For those God foreknew he also predestined *to be conformed to the likeness of his Son*" (author's emphasis). We could spend hours discussing and debating the exact definitions of "foreknew" and "predestined," but then we would miss the important point we need to understand for character development: God's plan is for us to be "conformed to the likeness of his Son." From the Lord's perspective, our becoming more like Jesus is a high priority.

In his book *The Life You've Always Wanted*, John Ortberg poses the question, How would you respond if someone asked you, "How is your spiritual life going these days?" Ortberg says,

> For many years I thought about this only in terms of a few special activities. If someone asked me how my spiritual life was going, my first thought would be how I was doing at having a quiet time— praying and reading the Bible each day. If I had prayed and read the Bible for several consecutive prior days, I was likely to say that my spiritual life was going well. If not, I was likely to feel guilty and downcast. So prayer and Bible study became the gauge of my spiritual condition.[1]

Ortberg recognizes that the key concern is not simply prayer and Bible study. I am not suggesting that prayer and Bible study are unimportant. We will discuss the necessity of each at length later in this book. However, those disciplines are simply a partial means to the end. The real goal— the final hoped-for outcome—is to become more like Jesus.

The apostle Paul says this about maturing in the Lord: "We will no longer be infants...we will in all things grow up into him, who is the Head, that is, Christ" (Ephesians 4:14–15). Like the little boy being selfish, it is time for us to live out that which we already know to be true. It's time to leave infancy behind. It's time to grow up. The goal of this book is to offer practical, tangible, biblical teaching that will help Christ-like character to be built in us.

It should be noted that you may find yourself becoming uncomfortable as you read—especially in the chapters that talk about specific character qualities. You may well recognize that from a biblical perspective you don't measure up. That's good. That means the Holy Spirit is at work bringing conviction in your life. Don't give up. The Spirit is still at work in you.

Conviction should not be confused with condemnation. Your job is to repent, ask for forgiveness, and ask God to cause you to do better in the future. Remember, the Lord desires that Christ-likeness be developed in your life even more than you do.

Additionally, it should be understood that this book is not meant to offer criteria whereby you may judge the character of another. Rather, it will most likely be a means by which God will demonstrate to each of us how far short we fall and how desperately we need Him and His mercy and grace.

I have tried to offer here a practical understanding of godly character. I have made every effort to base all that I say firmly on Scripture and to make it as applicable to your life as possible. I highly encourage you to check out everything I say for yourself. Don't just take my word for it. On that great last day, God is not going to ask you what *I* taught but what *you* believed. "Now the Bereans were of more noble character than the Thessalonians, for they received the message with great eagerness and *examined the Scriptures every day to see if what Paul said was true*" (Acts 17:11, author's emphasis). Start exercising some noble character by checking out for yourself what the Bible says about these things.

CHAPTER 2

CHARACTER—WHAT'S INSIDE?

Not long ago I read an article a woman wrote about her father. She described him as a very humble man who was always helping others. She shared several examples of the impact her father's life had on those around him. Then she told how, when he died, she took his old pocket watch to a jeweler to have it cleaned. The jeweler was fascinated by what he found when he opened its case. He explained that years ago it was possible to choose the case and the watch's works separately. Most people chose a fancy case but inferior works. They wanted people to be impressed by the fanciness of their watch, even though it was actually pretty shoddy inside. This watch was just the opposite. It had a very modest case, but the inner works were the best available. The writer realized that the watch was just like her dad—modest on the outside but the very best on the inside.

For us, perhaps the more important question is this: What does it mean to be more Christ-like?

As people—especially God's people—what we are like inside is far more important than what we look like on the outside. Our character is of much greater value than physical attractiveness. Even the secular world is beginning to recognize this concept more and more. I recently saw a billboard for the Boy Scouts of America. It said simply, "Strong Values. Strong Leaders. Character Counts." Of course it does.

James Emery White, in his book *You Can Experience a Purposeful Life*, shared this true story:

> Whenever there is a separation between values and practice, things break down. In ancient China, the people desired security from the barbaric, invading hordes to the north. To get this protection, they built the Great Wall of China.

It's 30 feet high, 18 feet thick, and more than 1,500 miles long!

The Chinese goal was to build an absolutely impenetrable defense—too high to climb over, too thick to break down, and too long to go around. But during the first hundred years of the wall's existence China was successfully invaded *three times*.

It wasn't the wall's fault. During all three invasions, the barbaric hordes never climbed over the wall, broke it down, or went around it; they simply bribed a gatekeeper and then marched right in through an open door. The purpose of the wall failed because of a breakdown in values.[1]

Because the gatekeepers did not exhibit godly character, the nation was imperiled. The dictionary defines character as "the group of ethical and mental characteristics that mark a person or group such as moral integrity; reputation."

In the Old Testament, when Boaz was attempting to pay Ruth the highest compliment he could, he did not refer to her beauty. Although Scripture seems to indicate that Ruth was a very beautiful woman, Boaz's comment was much deeper. He told Ruth, "All my fellow townsmen know that you are a woman of noble character" (Ruth 3:11). From Boaz's position the outward beauty was far less significant than the inward beauty, her character.

The Bible does not frequently use the term character, but it does describe it for us. "Make it your ambition to lead a quiet life, to mind your own business and to work with your hands, just as we told you, so that your daily life may win the respect of outsiders" (1 Thessalonians 4:11–12). *So that your daily life may win the respect of outsiders*. Character. How we live.

As Christians, we see Jesus as God's holy Son. His life, death, and resurrection have given us abundant life here and eternal life in the hereafter. To us He is everything. However, there are those who are not Christians—even some who are anti-Christian—who still hold the life of Jesus in high regard. Why?

Of course, it is partly because He was such a profound and practical teacher. Beyond that, though, the reason Jesus is so revered is because of His life and ideals. He was kind and compassionate, yet He stood up for what He believed. He was gentle and caring but refused to yield even before the haughty and arrogant religious leaders of His day. Jesus clearly epitomized servanthood and yet brazenly cleared the temple of those who were degrading God's house. He cared little for what others thought of Him. His desire was to follow His Father's will.

Jesus' life has been emulated by Christians and non-Christians for centuries, and rightly so. In our generation, the pivotal phrase from Charles Sheldon's classic book, *In His Steps*, has been popularized to the point of being a fad. "What would Jesus do?" can be seen on hats, t-shirts, bracelets, bumper stickers and notebook covers.

Perhaps the more important question for us is this: What does it mean to be more Christ-like? More than just how Jesus might behave in a particular situation, our lives should reflect His character. You know the old saying, "Actions speak louder than words." It's true. Our actions demonstrate who we really are far more than our words ever will. The Bible tells us, "Even a child is known by his actions, by whether his conduct is pure and right" (Proverbs 20:11).

More than asking in each situation how Jesus would respond, what we really need are moment-by-moment virtuous qualities that show forth *Who* He really is.

C.S. Lewis said it this way:

> Someone who is not a good tennis player may now and then make a good shot. What you mean by a good player is the man whose eye and muscles and nerves have been so trained by making innumerable good shots that they can now be relied on. They have a certain tone or quality which is there even when he is not playing, just as a mathematician's mind has a certain habit and outlook which is there even when he is not doing mathematics. In the same way a man who perseveres in doing just actions gets in the end a certain quality of character. Now it is that quality rather than the particular actions which we mean when we talk of 'virtue'.[2]

At this point you may be wondering, "Is it actually possible to display those virtuous character qualities in all of life?" The answer really depends on your perspective on the question. If you mean, "Is it possible to live the perfect life that Jesus lived?," of course the answer would have to be, "Not likely." However, if you mean, "Is it possible to develop a life that truly reflects the character of God through our everyday actions?," then my answer would be an emphatic "Yes!"

We all inherit traits from our earthly parents. My children all have very distinctive Kraeuter (*Kroy´-ter*) looks. Friends we haven't seen in years almost always look at my kids and then at me and say something like, "It's obvious whose children they are." Besides the physical appearance, there are also personality traits passed on to the next generation. My son Stephen acts so much like I did when I was a kid that I frequently telephone my mother and say, "Mom, I'm so sorry." She'll laugh and, in a very matter-of-fact way, ask, "What did Stephen do now, dear?" All of us inherit certain traits from our parents. What traits would you like to inherit from your heavenly Father?

Obtaining godly character is not something that occurs suddenly... Almost always it takes much more time than we would like for it to take.

I remember an early Amy Grant song entitled "My Father's Eyes." The song said that when people looked at her life, she wanted them to recognize that she had her Father's eyes. She wanted to have eyes that always looked for the good in each situation. She longed for eyes that showed compassion.

Obtaining godly character is not something that occurs suddenly, however. You are not likely to wake up one morning and find that you have taken on the fullness of godly character overnight. It takes time. Usually lots of time. Almost always it takes much more time than we would like for it to take.

I use a Bible program on my computer. One feature I have frequently found very helpful is *The Teacher's Commentary*. That commentary describes character development this way:

> We would all like to be instantaneously zapped
> with complete sanctification, to be sinless and
> perfect in everything we do. Unfortunately,
> although God could certainly cause that to hap-
> pen, generally He doesn't. Our maturation
> process is just that: a process. It takes time and
> growth is generally slow.[3]

Although it takes time to develop virtuous character, God has given us clear instructions in His Word that we should indeed act in a Christ-like manner. Paul prayed for the church at Colosse that they would "live a life worthy of the Lord and may please him in every way" (Colossians 1:10a). God would not ask us to do something if it were completely impossible. On the contrary, the Lord has shown us how He causes that Christ-like character to be formed in us. This book will give you practical tools for allowing God to build that Christ-likeness in your life, so that even upon close examination, your "inner workings" will be of the very best quality.

$\mathcal{C}$HARACTER PERMEATES A PERSON

There are two ways to make something a particular color or pattern of colors. One way is by topically applying a covering, such as paint. The other way is for the color to be an intrinsic part of the item. Purple plastic, for example, is not only purple on the surface; if you cut it, you will find it is purple to the core.

Over the years I have owned several shirts made of patterned material. In some the pattern was woven into the cloth. In others it was merely printed onto the surface. My experience has been that shirts made from printed material lose their colors much more quickly than those whose color pattern is actually in the weave.

In the same way, God is not interested in giving us a mere coating of a few attractive character qualities. Although that would make us look nice for awhile, over the long haul those topically applied qualities won't last.

My wife and I recently went shopping for a dresser for our youngest son. We found out there are essentially four types of "wood" furniture. The first, and most obvious, is furniture made from pieces of actual lumber, glued, screwed, nailed, or pegged together. The next step down from real wood furniture is wood veneer. The surface of this type of furniture is made from very thin pieces of wood, but they cover a chassis of particle board or plywood. After this comes laminate veneer, a combination of wood and epoxy or polyurethane also covering a main body made of something other than real wood. The least expensive type of "wood" furniture really contains very little actual wood. The surface is, in essence, a photograph of real wood glued onto particle board. From a distance (and when brand new) all of these can look very nice. The differences become evident in two ways: close inspection and wear and tear over time.

God wants to build character qualities into His people that hold up under close inspection. He desires us to have not just a surface covering that looks nice but honest, godly characteristics permeating our being. This type of character will not only endure the test of time but be enhanced by years of use.

Godly character is not generally an isolated part of a person, like a surface coat of paint. Character is usually something that permeates an individual.

This is not to suggest, however, that a person with true godly character could not have a major character flaw. The flesh, upbringing, education, and experiences in life will all affect what we are like. Alcoholic parents, major traumatic experiences, or bad habits developed in childhood can still cause serious flaws in an otherwise godly character. Someone whom the Lord has taken a very long way down the road of sanctification may still have some old baggage in a certain area. For example, a Christian brother who overall exhibits honesty and a servant attitude, as well as many other godly character qualities, may still have a problem with his temper or with lust.

> *A person who has not developed godly character over time will not generally display that type of behavior in a crisis situation.*

Clearly God is at work in his life, but he's not perfect. Ultimately, all character flaws are directly related to sin. It may even have been someone else's sin that started a flaw, but now it is part of that person's character.

Many books have been written and many sermons preached on the issue of godly character. A common Scripture text for such teaching is Galatians 5:22–23: "But the fruit of the Spirit is love, joy, peace, patience, kindness, goodness, faithfulness, gentleness and self-control." Each of these aspects of the fruit of the Spirit are definitely worth considering independently. However, it seems to me that to stop with looking at each individually would be to miss a very important aspect of this passage. Galatians 5:19–23 contrasts "the acts of the sinful nature" with "the fruit of the Spirit." "Acts" is plural. The acts of the sinful nature are a hodgepodge mixture. They are not necessarily connected. "Fruit," on the other hand, is singular. The fruit of the Spirit is not a bunch of different qualities but rather one thing with various aspects. God is not interested in simply layering a few nice character traits onto our lives. He wants His own unified character to permeate our beings.

A friend of mine, Brian Brasher, is a teacher at the Christian school affiliated with our church. Several years ago Brian was part of a short-term mission trip to Russia. On the return trip to Alaska, the small plane in which the group was flying ran out of fuel and crashed into the Bering Sea. When the first rescue helicopter arrived on the scene they went to Brian first. As the helicopter hovered into position to pull him out of the water, Brian realized that another man on his ministry team was close to giving up. The extended period of time in the 36-degree water had taken its toll. Delaying (and perhaps even forfeiting) his own chance to get out of the water, Brian waved the helicopter on toward the other man. A single heroic act? An isolated case of displaying godly character? Not likely. A person who has not developed godly character over time will not generally display that type of behavior in a crisis situation.

This past winter the administrator of the school where Brian teaches told me about a totally unrelated incident. Our area was hit with a snow storm. Although not rare in St. Louis, snow is certainly not common either. The administrator went to school a bit earlier than usual (and he is generally the first to arrive anyway) to make sure everything would be ready for the day. When he arrived, Brian and his new wife, Reneé, were shoveling the sidewalks. No one had asked them to do it. It was certainly not part of Brian's job description. It was simply a job that needed to be done, and they did it. I said this incident was totally unrelated to the first, but was it? Whether it was going the extra mile to shovel snow, or passing the rescue line on to someone who needed it more, Brian's character was to think of others.

True godly character can generally be seen across the board in a person's life, an intrinsic part of the whole person. Like fabric whose patterns are woven in, or furniture made of real wood, we want our lives to be a quality product. We want to bear that fruit of the Spirit. In moments of crisis, we want our lives to reflect the character of Christ that permeates our person.

CHAPTER 4

WHAT YOU DO VS. WHO YOU ARE

The concept of godly character is really quite foreign to our society. We are more likely to look at what people do than who they are. We value achievement far more highly than character. When two people first meet, what is the most common initial question? "What do you do for a living?" The answer often determines how much further the conversation goes. Professional athlete or actor, politician or cartoonist, are all careers we deem worth discussing. However, let someone mention that they are a check-out clerk or a garbage collector and we quickly change the topic. The sad part is that we often miss the bigger point: *who* that person is. What they are really like as a person is far more important than what they do for a living.

Unfortunately, this achievement ideology has carried over into the kingdom of God. Christians who *do* great things are esteemed. Those through whom God has performed great miracles, those who are highly "anointed"—who have the apparent touch of God on their lives and ministries—are valued far more than those who have been quietly and faithfully doing God's work for decades.

> *This issue of character is not, as some might suggest, a peripheral issue. What we are like as people directly reflects what we believe.*

Several years ago I heard a powerful statement that really struck me. "The anointing—that special touch from God that allows us to transcend the natural—on the life of a believer proves only one thing: God is faithful to His promises. It says nothing about the character and life of that person." It's true. You can look at some people in our generation alone who did miraculous things in the Name of the Lord Jesus Christ but whose lives were a complete sham. Not all who are powerfully touched by God are like that, but too many are.

Mighty works do not indicate that a person has godly character. God used a donkey to rescue Balaam (Numbers 22:21–40). God used a hard-hearted high priest named Caiaphas to prophesy that Jesus would die for the Jewish nation (John 11:49–51). God miraculously used evil kings to subdue His rebellious people. The miraculous touch of God on a person does not mean that God is pleased with their character. In fact, the Lord seems almost shameless about whom He will use to accomplish His purposes.

However, how we live—what we are really like as people—is far more important to God than all the miraculous works we can ever perform. Do you remember Jesus' Sermon on the Mount? In the most extended biblical account of that message (Matthew 5–7), Jesus spends most of three chapters discussing everyday life. How they should live was His primary topic. It is here that He delivers the powerful imperative, "Let your light shine before men, that they may see your good deeds and praise your Father in heaven" (Matthew 5:16). In the Greek "good deeds" does not refer to miracles. It is simply the everyday things of life. How we live. *Vine's Expository Dictionary* says that this word "frequently occurs in an ethical sense of human actions, good or bad." God wants others to see that we are different from them in our daily lives in order that they might glorify Him. And that is just one verse. For two and a half chapters Jesus pours into the people example after example of how they should live.

Finally, toward the end of chapter seven, Jesus makes a statement that many of us know but few of us understand in context. "Many will say to Me on that day, 'Lord, Lord, did we not prophesy in your name...and perform many miracles?' Then I will tell them plainly, 'I never knew you.

Away from me you evildoers!'" (Matthew 7:22–23). If you read this in the context of the entire sermon, Jesus is clearly saying, "It's not just the great miracles I'm interested in. It's how you live your life that is really important."

For us as Christians this issue of character is not, as some might suggest, a peripheral issue. Paul, the apostle, said, "You must teach what is in accord with sound doctrine. Teach the older men to be temperate, worthy of respect, self-controlled" (Titus 2:1–2). He goes on to talk about similar ideas regarding older women, younger women, younger men, and even slaves. Paul is clearly equating sound doctrine (v. 1) with issues of character. This is not a side issue to the "important stuff." What we are like as people directly reflects what we believe.

So far we have only considered the character issue from a general perspective. However, unless we have a really clear picture of what character should be like, we may not know if we are getting close to the goal. In the next several chapters we will discuss the specifics of what godly character should look like in everyday life.

CHAPTER 5

THE BUSINESS OF INTEGRITY

I just heard a report on the news about a nineteen-year-old computer hacker. He was a well educated honor student who was arrested for breaking into the computer systems of some of the nation's largest companies. This young man was very proficient at what he did. The FBI said there was no computer in the world that was safe from him.

Our culture tries to tell us that if we will educate people enough then they will do the right thing. The idea is that somehow information will make people good. The reality is that this way of thinking is completely wrong. The young hacker was well educated, but he had no integrity.

Integrity. That's an elusive idea and often foreign to our society. Webster defines integrity as "strict adherence to a standard of value or conduct." The Hebrew words that are generally translated as integrity in our English Bibles literally mean "uprightness" or "perfection." In the current vernacular we might say, "Doing the right thing." The words integrity and character can almost be used interchangeably, but integrity seems a bit more specific. It implies forthrightness in our dealings with one another, with no underhandedness.

> *After running up a debt of thousands of dollars, a Christian organization began patronizing a competitor on a cash-only basis.*

When Joash was king of Israel (2 Kings 12), he initiated a major restoration of the temple. It is interesting to read all the job entailed and how much money was involved. Yet an intriguing statement was made about those who took care of the money: "They did not require an accounting from those to whom they gave the money to pay the workers, because they acted with complete honesty"! (2 Kings 12:15). Can you imagine how we would receive such a statement today? "You're asking for trouble.

There are no safeguards." That's because our society overall has little integrity.

Unfortunately, lack of integrity can also be found among Christians. Recently I recognized this anew when some Christian businessmen friends of mine got "burned." They stuck their necks out for fellow believers and nearly got their heads chopped off. The first, sales manager for a small company, was dealt with in a very inequitable way by a large church. He almost refinanced his home to pay off his company's loss because he did not want his boss to bear the brunt of unethical treatment by the church. My friend would rather suffer personally than cause the name of Christ to be slandered.

The second friend owns his own business. One of his largest customers is a Christian organization. After running up a debt of thousands of dollars with my friend they began patronizing a competitor on a cash-only basis. These sorts of dealings are absolutely inexcusable! I have talked with numerous businessmen across the nation who have told me they would rather deal with a secular company than a church or church-related ministry because of this lack of integrity.

In contrast, consider the apostle Paul and his companions. They had collected a large offering from various churches to be distributed among the poor. Paul was very careful in his handling of the money to be certain that no one could accuse him of financial misappropriation. He told the church at Corinth, "We want to avoid any criticism of the way we administer this liberal gift. For we are taking pains to do what is right, not only in the eyes of the Lord but also in the eyes of men" (2 Corinthians 8:20–21).

In general, it seems that integrity is too often lacking in the Church. We say we are pursuing the things of God, but at what expense? Do we leave behind a scandalous trail of inequitable dealings with the world? Do we blatantly wrong a brother or sister in Christ and not have the slightest twinge of remorse? Are these godly attitudes? It is time for the Church to stop dragging the name of the Lord through the mud by the way we treat people. Too often we say with our mouths, "I love God," while our actions say, "I don't care about you at all." What kind of a witness is that to the world? What kind of "love" is that to show to a brother? (See 1 John 4:20–21.)

David said, "I know, my God, that you test the heart and are pleased with integrity" (1 Chronicles 29:17). The Lord places a high priority on how we interact with one another. His Word is clear: "The man of integrity walks securely, but he who takes crooked paths will be found out" (Proverbs 10:9).

Are your business practices above reproach? Are you able to say that your actions are right in all your dealings with others, "not only in the eyes of the Lord but also in the eyes of men"? Do you have integrity?

THE IMPORTANCE OF PROMISES KEPT

W hen the Israelites were entering the promised land, God had clearly instructed them to destroy all of the inhabitants. Because the people of Israel were so obviously intent on wiping them out, some of the natives of the land banded together in armed opposition against them. However, one group, the Gibeonites, took a different course of action. They staged a deception.

It was actually quite a clever ruse. They loaded donkeys with "worn-out sacks and old wine-skins, cracked and mended. The men put worn and patched sandals on their feet and wore old clothes. All of the bread of their food supply was dry and moldy. Then they went to Joshua in the camp at Gilgal and said to him and the men of Israel, 'We have come from a distant country; make a treaty with us'" (Joshua 9:4–6). The deception was so effective that Joshua and company agreed to make a treaty and not destroy them. The Israelites promised to allow the people of Gibeon to live.

> *God desires someone who will stand by what he promised, even if what he has promised will hurt him.*

When the people of Israel realized the truth, they were outraged and wanted to destroy the Gibeonites. The Israelite leaders, however, refused to allow it because they had already promised not to kill them. Instead, the people of Gibeon became wood cutters and water carriers for the Israelites.

Hold on a minute! God wanted those people destroyed. He had very clearly told Israel that all the inhabitants were to be killed. The Gibeonites had resorted to trickery to keep themselves from being destroyed. Because of this deception, the Israelite leaders had promised to allow them to live. Was this okay with God? Let's take a look.

We are going to fast-forward in history to the time of King David. "During the reign of David, there was a famine for three successive years; so David sought the face of the

LORD. The LORD said, 'It is on account of Saul and his bloodstained house; it is because he put the Gibeonites to death'" (2 Samuel 21:1). Saul, in his zeal for Israel and Judah, had tried to annihilate the people of Gibeon even though Israel had a treaty with them. Because Saul had broken the treaty, God brought a three-year famine on the nation of Israel.

Get the picture here. The Gibeonites had used deceit to trick the Israelites into agreeing to allow them to live. This agreement was completely contrary to God's instructions. Yet later the Lord is obviously displeased with Saul for breaking the treaty. Therein lies a lesson for us: God places a very high value on living up to our promises.

Psalm 15 is one of the shortest chapters in the Bible. It is only five verses long, but those verses are very potent. The psalm starts by asking a couple of questions: "LORD, who may dwell in your sanctuary? Who may live on your holy hill?" In essence David is asking, "God, what type of people do You want around You?" The remainder of the psalm lists several character qualities that the Lord desires in our lives.

Recently, as I read this section of Scripture, one of those character qualities stood out to me. It talks about someone "who keeps an oath even when it hurts" (v. 4b). Other translators state it like this:

> "and is true, come what may, to his pledged word" (Ronald Knox).
> "One who will keep a promise, even to his own detriment, and will not retract" (R.K. Harrison).

What this verse is saying is that one of the character qualities God wants to see in His people is honesty. He desires someone who will stand by what he promised, even if what he has promised will hurt him. In our society this is a very foreign concept. Our western culture tells us, "Look out for number one." We find it perfectly acceptable to alter the truth to keep ourselves from getting hurt. Given the choice, most people would rather lie than bring harm to themselves by telling the truth. This is not God's way.

Even in the Church this idea of being true to our word is too often outside of our normal thinking. I cannot even recall all the times I have been burned by Christians who said they were going to do something and, when it came time to do it, suddenly backed out because it was no longer convenient—no matter that they had already promised to do it. They changed their mind.

Please understand that I am not sharing this from a position of "sour grapes." It is not simply because promises were broken to *me* that I find this important. I am far more concerned about how this issue looks from God's perspective. Jesus depicted the heart of the Father when He said, "Whatever you did for one of the least of these brothers of Mine, you did for Me" (Matthew 25:40). If we do not keep our promises to one another, it is as though we have not kept our promises to the Lord. Can you fathom this same God watching us go back on our word—reneging on our promises—and smiling approvingly? I think not.

Another incident occurred later in Israel's history that further demonstrates God's heart on this issue. Amaziah, king of Judah, was preparing his people to go into battle. He had mustered 300,000 soldiers, and Scripture tells us that "He also hired a hundred thousand fighting men from Israel for a hundred talents of silver" (2 Chronicles 25:6).

God was not pleased with Amaziah's decision, however. "But a man of God came to him and said, 'O king, these troops from Israel must not march with you, for the LORD is not with Israel—not with any of the people of Ephraim. Even if you go and fight courageously in battle, God will overthrow you before the enemy, for God has the power to help or to overthrow'" (2 Chronicles 25:7–8).

What a dilemma! Amaziah had already plunked down what would today be the equivalent of more than $1,000,000. So what was he to do? "Amaziah asked the man of God, 'But what about the hundred talents I paid for these Israelite troops?'" (2 Chronicles 25:9a). That was a fair question. He didn't want to just throw the money away. However, he had already made a commitment. What should he do?

Sometimes we make rash, not-too-well-thought-out commitments. God would have us follow through—even if it means getting hurt in the process.

"The man of God replied, 'The LORD can give you much more than that'" (2 Chronicles 25:9b). Notice that there is no mention of the possibility of a refund from Israel. The prophet of God did not suggest that Israel would act like Wal-Mart and cheerfully give back the money for any reason. He also did not tell Amaziah to have his 300,000 men go and take the money back. In essence what the man of God was saying was,

"Don't worry about it. God can more than make up the loss. Trust Him and stand by your word."

"So Amaziah dismissed the troops who had come to him from Ephraim and sent them home" (2 Chronicles 25:10). That was undoubtedly a difficult decision for Amaziah. He just sent 25% of his troops home with more than one million dollars in pay for doing nothing. He honored his commitment, however, and he knew that God could return, as the prophet had said, "much more than that."

Sometimes we too make rash, not-too-well-thought-out commitments. Rather than seeing us go back on our word, though, God would have us follow through—even if it means our getting hurt in the process—being, as David said, one "who keeps an oath even when it hurts" (Psalm 15:4b). From God's perspective being true to our word is an important commodity.

I recently heard about a Christian school that had applied to several foundations for $24,000 grants to purchase new playground equipment. Because so many people apply for such grants, the chance of actually receiving money is slim. In an unusual twist, two of the foundations approved the school for the funds. It received not one but two checks, each for $24,000, to purchase the playground equipment. When the school realized what had happened, they were faced with a dilemma. Should they keep both checks and create a playground far more elaborate than what they had originally envisioned, or should they stick with what they had proposed? When they honestly considered the situation, they realized there really wasn't any dilemma at all. They had requested money to complete a specific project. To go beyond what they had proposed would be dishonest. They returned one of the checks.

Suppose you had the opportunity to meet with James, the brother of Jesus who apparently presided over the council of Jerusalem (Acts 15). If you had just a few minutes with James and could ask him what he thought was really important for us to understand in this life, what do you think he would say? Actually James already told us what he thought was most important when he wrote, *"Above all,* my brothers, do not swear—not by heaven or by earth or by anything else. Let your 'Yes' be yes, and your 'No,' no, or you will be condemned" (James 5:12, author's emphasis). What James is saying is, "Be true to your word." He is telling us that our word should be so reliable that there is no need to reinforce it by swearing by anything more. Your word should be enough.

> *"Dave, that tells me a whole lot about your character. You would rather put yourself out than to go back on your word."*

I have a dear friend who lives across the street from me. One day he called and asked me to take him to the repair shop to pick up his car. I thought this was a strange request because I knew they owned two automobiles, but I agreed to take him.

On the way to the shop I found out why he had called. He had loaned their other car to someone who was having car trouble. While this other person had the car, my friend also had car trouble—with his one remaining automobile. "I thought about asking for our car to be returned," said my friend, "but I had already promised them they could use it."

My response was immediate, "Dave, that tells me a whole lot about your character. You would rather put yourself out than to go back on your word." As Christians we need that type of attitude.

In a culture where the idea of absolute truth has been abandoned, this way of thinking appears outlandish. Most people would say, "Situations and circumstances change. Certainly I can't be expected to keep *all* of my promises." But look at that line of thought from a purely logical perspective. If you tell me that it is acceptable to go back on your word under certain circumstances, then why should I believe anything you tell me? Jesus said it just like James (hmmm, I wonder if that might be where James got it): "Simply let your 'Yes' be 'Yes,' and your 'No,' 'No'" (Matthew 5:37).

Being true to our word is not just a good idea. It is a strong scriptural mandate. Are we completely honest? Are we committed to keeping our promises—no matter what? Let's be people that are true to what we say, even if it causes us difficulty.

CHAPTER 7

THE STRENGTH OF GENTLENESS

Scripture tells us to "clothe" ourselves with gentleness (Colossians 3:12) and to "pursue" gentleness (1 Timothy 6:11). It even says, "Let your gentleness be evident to all" (Philippians 4:5). Gentleness is a difficult thing to define precisely. Oh, we all have a general idea of what it means to be gentle, but *exactly* what it means in each situation can get a little tricky. However, I know for certain that gentleness is not weakness.

I'll let you in on a little secret. I'm a chocolate fanatic. I enjoy really good chocolate. So does most of the rest of my family. One of our family favorites is Dove® Promises, small chocolate candies, individually wrapped, with an oftentimes quotable quote inside the wrapper. I purchase them because of the quality of chocolate, not for the memorable sayings, but recently I was savoring a few of these tasty morsels and noticed a profound statement inside one of the wrappers: "Nothing is as strong as gentleness or as gentle as strength."

Although I would certainly never place a candy wrapper anywhere close to the level of Scripture, this statement is extremely accurate. Although these two concepts—gentleness and strength—seem contradictory, they really are intrinsically tied together. Proverbs 15:1 informs us, "A gentle answer turns away wrath." This passage does not suggest that we use force to turn away wrath. Rather, being gentle will diffuse the anger.

In her eight brief years on earth, my daughter has frequently crossed the line of acceptable behavior. On those occasions she knows she must face the consequences. Upon realizing she is in trouble, however, more than once she has looked at me very sweetly and said, "I love you, Daddy." Although she has still been punished, the consequences have probably been less severe. Her gentleness diffused my anger. There really is not anything as strong as gentleness.

I am relatively certain that you are at least somewhat familiar with the story of Jesus washing His disciples' feet. There is a little two-letter word that you may not have noticed, though, that gives meaning to the entire scenario.

"Jesus knew that the Father had put all things under his power, and that he had come from God and was returning to God; so he got up from the meal, took off his outer clothing, and wrapped a towel around his waist...and began to wash his disciples' feet" (John 13:3–5).

Did you catch it? It's the word "so." "Jesus knew that the Father had put all things under His power, and that He had come from God and was returning to God; *so* He got up..." Jesus knew He was all-powerful. In a brief time He was headed back to His real home. He was God. *So* He did not need to prove Himself. *So* He did not need to lord it over His disciples. Because He had the strength to do anything, He could afford to be gentle. *So* He washed His disciples' feet. There really is not anything as gentle as true strength.

> *Throughout His life when He was mocked, ridiculed, reviled, scorned, laughed at, not believed, called "the devil," beaten, hit, and finally, nailed to a cross, Jesus was gentle.*

In his letter to the church at Ephesus, Paul tells us to, "Be completely humble and gentle" (Ephesians 4:2a). To be honest, I wish this verse did not say "completely." Occasionally I know how to be humble and gentle, but the Greek word translated "completely" is all-inclusive. It appears to indicate that we should be gentle all the time in all situations. I really do not like that idea. For much of my life I have been very assertive. I want my way. Oh, I know how to be gentle now and then, but all the time?! This seems a bit much.

Jesus came to earth not only to die for our sins but to be an example for our lives (John 13:15, 1 Corinthians 11:1). In Matthew's account of the life of Jesus, our Savior said, "Take my yoke upon you and learn from me, for I am gentle and humble in heart" (Matthew 11:29). We should learn from Jesus' example. Throughout His life, when He was mocked, ridiculed, reviled, scorned, laughed at, not believed, called "the devil," beaten, hit, and finally, nailed to a cross, Jesus was gentle. No personal attack ever caused Him to be anything less than gentle.

It should be understood that gentleness is not commanded only for our own sakes. Others around us need us to be gentle, just as we need them to be gentle with us. Not long ago I happened across an article by author Gary L. Thomas. He said it this way:

> I was working on my car—always a frustrating experience for a mechanical klutz like me—and my youngest was keeping me company. As she inspected my tools, she opened my socket set—upside down. Sixty-four sockets rolled onto the sidewalk.
>
> "Oh, Kelsey," I said. I didn't yell or even raise my voice. But she is so sensitive that just the tone was enough to elicit a pained expression. She started to walk toward the house.
>
> "Kelsey?"
>
> She turned.
>
> "You didn't mean to do that. I'm not angry at you. It's all right."

> Kelsey broke down, ran back to me, and buried
> her face in my shoulder. Her actions reminded me
> how easily people are wounded. On the outside,
> everybody looks fine. But inside, many are bruised
> reeds just waiting to topple over.[1]

Too often we end up mangling those bruised reeds when we act in a less-than-gentle manner.

Although it is especially important for us to be gentle with our brothers and sisters in Christ, we should also be gentle with unbelievers. Our gentleness—or lack thereof—may mean the difference of someone spending eternity in heaven or hell. "Always be prepared to give an answer to everyone who asks you to give the reason for the hope that you have. But do this with gentleness" (1 Peter 3:15).

What about you? Are you *always* gentle? Do you have a tendency to sound off at others about their mistakes? Is gentleness lacking in your life? Ask God right now to cause you to become more gentle in every situation.

CHAPTER 8

THE CONSISTENCY OF KINDNESS

Our church has a Christian school, grades K through 12. A few years ago many of our elementary students were involved in a multischool track and field competition. One young lady, Chrissy Branch, a sixth-grader, was competing in a distance race and had a good chance of winning; she is quite athletic and *very* competitive. However, not far from the beginning of the race one of her competitors from another school slipped and fell. Chrissy stopped, went back, helped the girl up, and walked with her for the rest of the race. She gave up her own chance of winning in order to show kindness to someone else. It was a simple act of kindness but one of a kind that is all too rare in our culture.

Paul wrote to the Thessalonian believers, "Always try to be kind to each other and to everyone else" (1 Thessalonians 5:15). Paul didn't say to be kind "once in a while" or "when you feel like it." Always means always. This verse also indicates that we should be willing to put forth effort. The Greek word that is translated as "try" literally means to "pursue" or "follow after." It suggests getting involved. Honestly trying to be kind may require work on our part.

> *Chrissy stopped, went back, helped the girl up, and walked with her for the rest of the race.*

The first half of this same verse may give us an indication of a practical application of trying to be kind. "Make sure that nobody pays back wrong for wrong" (1 Thessalonians 5:15). The last time someone wronged you, what was your immediate reaction? Kindness? If not then perhaps it's time to begin to expend the necessary energy to "always try to be kind."

Joseph, the earthly father of Jesus, demonstrated kindness in the way he intended to deal with his fiancé. Although God later spoke to Joseph in a dream, Joseph apparently found out about the baby first from Mary. Unfortunately he didn't believe her story about an angelic visitation. He did not use that as an excuse to act in an unkind manner toward her, however. "Because Joseph her husband was a righteous man and did not want to expose her to public disgrace, he had in mind to divorce her quietly" (Matthew 1:19).

Get the picture here. A betrothed woman being "with child" was a disgrace beyond measure in this society. Joseph knew for certain that he was not the father and therefore had every right to make a public spectacle of Mary. But he was "a righteous man," and that made all the difference. Please understand that quietly breaking the engagement would not put an end to the matter. He would, of course, have to explain the broken engagement to friends and family. The disgrace and humiliation he would endure would be awful. Nevertheless, he refused to be unkind. Although he believed he had been wronged, he refused to pay back in like manner. He would handle the situation in a gentle, quiet, and kind manner. It was the right thing to do, and he would do it.

I like the bumper stickers that encourage people to do random acts of kindness. What a truly different world it would be if everyone looked for ways to be kind to one another. What if every professing Christian were kind to everyone they encountered? We could revolutionize the world's image of the Church overnight. Unfortunately I have met some very unkind Christians, and I am not talking about recent converts. Some who have been believers for years—even a few clergy—have displayed rudeness through unkind words and actions in a way that caused the recipients to recoil in disgust.

God's Word talks a lot about kindness. Colossians 3:12 tells us to clothe ourselves with several things, one of which is kindness. Ephesians 4:32 says bluntly, "Be kind."

Each day you and I are faced with a myriad of opportunities to be either kind or unkind. For example, how do we treat the person who physically bumps into us at the store. Or the belligerent co-worker? Or maybe the far-too-much-in-a-hurry person who cuts us off in traffic? Or even the child who—for the twentieth time—asks when grandma is coming? How do we respond in these situations? Do we act kindly?

> *The Lord seemed to remind me what a depraved state I had been in when God showered His kindness on me.*

I'll be honest. As I was finishing this particular chapter, I was staying in a hotel. The light over the sink did not work when I checked in, but I was already settled into the room when I realized it. I called the front desk and asked that they have it fixed as soon as possible. The next afternoon I asked again...and the following morning I asked a third time. Each time I was assured that it would be repaired soon. Unfortunately their promises did not make it any easier for me to see to shave—a somewhat difficult process in the dark. The longer this went on, the more unkind thoughts I began to have toward the hotel staff. I found it increasingly difficult to be kind. It was at that point that the Lord seemed to remind me what a depraved state I had been in when God showered *His* kindness on me. Recognizing that I had been the recipient of such immense kindness made it much easier for me to demonstrate kindness to others.

What about you? Have you also been the recipient of God's kindness? What would have happened if He had dealt with you in the way you deserved? Doesn't that realization make being kind to others a whole lot easier?

CHAPTER 9

THE DUTY OF DILIGENCE

Often the people in history (or even in our present day) that we admire are those who kept going over the long haul. They didn't quit when things got tough. I once heard a motivational speaker say, "The common denominator of nearly all successful people is that they learned to conquer the temptation to give up." Too often we prefer to take the easy way out. If it doesn't work the first time, many people's natural inclination is to give up. The idea of being diligent and persistent is not usually a natural way of thinking for us.

The Bible speaks much about the concepts of diligence and persistence. In Ezra's account of the rebuilding of Jerusalem, he talks five times about the work being done with "diligence." "Diligent hands will rule, but laziness ends in slave labor" (Proverbs 12:24). Jesus tells us that we should be persistent (Luke 11:8). Paul instructs Timothy to be diligent (1 Timothy 4:15). This idea pops up repeatedly throughout the pages of Scripture.

> *Future baseball Hall-of-Famer Ozzie Smith spent hours and hours, in his words, "relentlessly pursuing" his dream.*

Some time ago I read an interesting article. It talked about when McDonald's was first going to build a restaurant in Russia. With their resources they could easily have simply jumped in and built the restaurant. Instead they did research and careful planning.

When they discovered there was a shortage of almost everything, they went all the way back to the beginning of the process. They started wheat farms, then potato farms and tomato farms. Later they started their own bakeries. It took them 15 years, but when they finally opened they were hugely successful. Now there are

McDonald's sprouting up all over Moscow and other cities.[1]

This story reminds me a bit of Solomon's words: "Lazy hands make a man poor, but diligent hands bring wealth" (Proverbs 10:4). McDonald's diligence paid off. They could have been impetuous and simply dived in. Instead they did careful research and development. They were diligent in their efforts. It took longer, but it was definitely worth it in the end.

The Bible has some very strong words to say to those who are not diligent: "One who is slack in his work is brother to one who destroys" (Proverbs 18:9). "Brother to one who destroys"?! Many people in our society have a very lackadaisical attitude toward work, whether their job, chores around the home, schoolwork, or even their work for the kingdom of God. Their attitude may be, "I'm doing as much as the next guy." Unless we're honestly putting forth our best effort, however, the Bible says we are a brother to one who destroys. I, for one, do not want to be in that category.

Scripture tells us, "Let us not become weary in doing good, for at the proper time we will reap a harvest if we do not give up" (Galatians 6:9). This means we must work diligently and continue to work diligently.

Future baseball Hall-of-Famer Ozzie Smith played shortstop for the St. Louis Cardinals. He set numerous records during his illustrious career. Just after his retirement I heard him sharing about his childhood. He had dreamed of being a professional baseball player. He told how as a young boy he would throw a ball over the roof of his house and then run as fast as he could to the other side to field the ball. Smith said that he spent hours and hours doing that.

He also related that it was not just to kill time. He was, in his words, "relentlessly pursuing" his dream. It was obvious that the dream would not be fulfilled for many years, but he was prepared to pay the price of work and waiting to make it reality. He was very diligent in his efforts.

Undoubtedly Jesus is our best example of diligence and persistence. At any point in His life He could easily have quit. Especially in the days leading up to His crucifixion, the temptation to bail out must have been overwhelming. In the midst of those trying days we get some glimpses of Jesus' character.

"As the time approached for him to be taken up to heaven, Jesus *resolutely* set out for Jerusalem" (Luke 9:51, author's emphasis). There was no wavering on His part. He had made up His mind. Jesus was on His way to Jerusalem, where He knew He must lay down His life.

Later, in the Garden of Gethsemane, Jesus "fell with his face to the ground and prayed, 'My Father, if it is possible, may this cup be taken from me'" (Matthew 26:39). Obviously Jesus was in great agony. The emotional turmoil must have been almost unbearable. That's why He asked, "May this cup be taken from me." But Jesus didn't stop there. He went on to say, "Yet not as I will, but as you will." His immediate feelings and desires were important but not nearly as important as what He had come to do. He was determined to see this plan through to the very end. He would remain diligent in spite of the pain and suffering. As important as the difficulties were, they paled in comparison to the idea of just giving up. Jesus' persistence is a shining example for all of His followers.

I sometimes read sections of *The Living Bible* because it can offer a simple understanding of some verses. I really like the rendering of 2 Corinthians 4:8–9: "We are pressed on every side by troubles, but not crushed and broken. We are perplexed, but we don't give up and quit. We are hunted down, but God never abandons us. We get knocked down, but we get up again and keep going."

How about you? Do you faint at the first sign of opposition? Or are you diligent and persistent in all you do?

CHAPTER 10

THE FOUNDATION OF TRUTHFULNESS

Our Savior's emphasis on truth is unmistakable. We cannot read the gospel accounts and miss it. In Matthew's account alone, Jesus is quoted as saying, "I tell you the truth," thirty different times. Although from our perspective it would seem ludicrous to suggest that the holy Son of God might have lied, it also seems obvious that His consistent reference to telling the truth was to make a point: truthfulness is not an option; it is mandatory.

The apostle Paul said it like this: "Therefore each of you must put off falsehood and speak truthfully to his neighbor" (Ephesians 4:25). The words "each of you *must*" do not sound like a suggestion to me. Paul is insisting that we be consistently honest with one another.

Please recognize that I am not just talking about truthfulness in the big things. Maybe you were 100% honest in the million-dollar business transaction. That is commendable. However, did you tell the check-out clerk she had given you $1.00 too much change? Or did you take any questionable deductions on your latest tax return? Does your company know you took that box of paper clips? It is not just truthfulness in the big things that makes a difference.

> *Recent polls indicate that we as a people do not care in the least about whether our elected representatives lie to us (or to others) about their personal affairs.*

My wife and I have consistently endeavored to instill truthfulness into our children. The statement "It is *always* best to tell the truth" has been heard in our home many, many times over the years. As the kids have grown, we have explained to them that there will most likely come times when they will *need* for us to believe them. They may someday find themselves in an awkward position at school or with a friend. If at other times they have given us reason to doubt their truthfulness, it will be much more difficult to get us to believe their word in a crisis.

It is imperative to be completely honest and truthful in all our dealings, not just the big ones. This concept is unfamiliar in our society. Recent polls indicate that we as a people do not care in the least about whether our elected representatives lie to us (or to others) about their personal affairs. As long as they do a good job in their elected office, what our leaders do privately is their business. That sounds somewhat rational (unless of course you actually have a brain), but the final conclusion is obvious: If someone is willing to lie about one area, why would we even begin to think that they would not lie about another? The standard is complete truthfulness, or there really is no standard at all.

One practical way that we can make truthfulness a bit more of a reality in our lives is by recognizing that as Christians we are representatives of Christ. "You are not your own; you were bought at a price" (1 Cor 6:19b–20a). We do not belong to ourselves. Therefore all our words should honor God. Jesus phrased it like this: "He who speaks on his own does so to gain honor for himself, but he who works for the honor of the one who sent him is a man of truth; there is nothing false about him" (John 7:18).

Ephesians 6 describes the armor of God that every Christian should wear. Part of that armor is the belt of truth. Verse 14 tells us, "Stand firm then, with the belt of truth buckled around your waist." This translation gives the impression that the belt of truth is already there, buckled around our waist. Actually, the Greek implies action on our part. Literally it says to "gird about." That requires action on our part. We must actually do something with it. We must willingly take an active role in having truth be part of us.

Additionally, the Greek word that is translated as "waist" in Ephesians 6:14 seems to have been more accurately captured by the KJV as "loins." It has an outward as well as an inward connotation. David proclaimed, "Surely you desire truth in the inner parts" (Psalm 51:6a). Truth should not just be on the outside, but on the inside as well. It must be an intrinsic part of us, day in and day out.

How about you? Are your words to others completely honest? Do you ever stretch the truth a bit to your spouse or family? What about your boss or coworkers? Friends? Is truth an intrinsic part of *your* life?

CHAPTER 11

THE LOST ART
OF LOYALTY

S am Davis was a twenty-one-year-old Confederate sol-
dier who was captured behind Union lines. He chose
death rather than pardon when he refused to reveal
the name of his informant. His response was clear: "Do you
suppose that I would betray a friend? No, sir, I would die a
thousand times first." Such depth of loyalty and commitment are almost unheard of in our day and age. I would go

so far as to suggest that the overwhelming majority of people in our society, given the same choice, would reveal the name of the friend.

Some time ago I was listening to a radio talk show. "Loyalty? Commitment?! Those are foreign words from another era." The host's intensity increased as he continued, "We know nothing of those words in our society. Employers regularly lay off workers who have been with the company for decades. Employees leave their position—for which the company has diligently trained them—as soon as a better offer comes along. Teachers punch a time clock with little regard as to whether they have actually educated anyone. Spouses casually throw off wedding vows as though the words were never said. Military brass show no remorse as they are tried and convicted for selling national secrets. Police officers betray the law they have sworn to uphold. Loyalty? Commitment?! Not in this country. Not in this day and age."

> *Some time ago I was listening to a radio talk show. "Loyalty? Commitment?! Those are foreign words from another era."*

I sat stunned. I knew he was right, but I hated to admit it. My guess is that the average person in our society could not even begin to define those terms. At the very least, it seems safe to assume that the average definition would be light-years away from the sense we find of those concepts in Scripture.

It should be noted that neither of these words, loyalty nor commitment, are used extensively in the Bible. However, we can see a *demonstration* of these concepts again and again throughout the pages of God's Word.

Perhaps the most amazing example of godly loyalty and commitment is Moses. At one point his attempts to convince Pharaoh to let God's people go simply resulted in the Israelites being forced to do more work than ever. When this happened they turned against Moses and said, "May the LORD look upon you and judge you! You have made us a stench to Pharaoh and his officials and have put a sword in their hand to kill us" (Exodus 5:21).

What would you have done in this situation? Our reaction today would be something like, "I am certainly not going to continue to try to help those ungrateful wretches." However, even though his own people were vehemently opposing him, Moses continued to be committed to the mission God had given him. At a time when most men would have given up and walked away, Moses continued on.

A recent survey by George Barna discovered that 11% of those who attend a Christian church at least once a month plan to change their place of worship in the coming year. Barna concluded, "Despite their fascination with spirituality, most church people are only moderately devoted to their current church and they are not deeply invested in spiritual growth." H.B. London, Jr., of Focus on the Family, made this comment: "We, like trendy teenagers, seem to 'go where the action is'—follow the latest fad. We are a 'disposable society'—less inclined to loyalty."[1]

What a sad commentary. I can understand little or no commitment from the world. But from Christians?

Moses' obvious care for and loyalty to his people shone through even more brightly after Israel left Egypt. At the request of the people, Aaron made a golden calf for them to worship. God became very angry with the people and threatened to annihilate them and replace them with a nation from Moses' seed (Exodus 32:10). Moses' response is almost unbelievable: "Why should the Egyptians say, 'It was with evil intent that he brought them out, to kill them in the mountains and to wipe them off the face of the earth'? Turn from your fierce anger; relent and do not bring disaster on your people" (Exodus 32:12).

When I read stories of God's dealings with people in the Bible, I often try to imagine myself in their place. I consider what I might do in the same situation. In this case I am convinced that my response would have been quite different from Moses'. I probably would have thought how nice it would be to have my own nation. It would be wonderful to have people throughout history referring to *my* God as *the* God. After all, I would have rationalized, the people were guilty. God had every right to destroy them. They had seen His sovereign power lead them out of Egypt and sustain them until this time, and yet they suddenly decided they needed another god. The Lord could have wiped them from the face of the earth and been completely justified in doing it.

Fortunately, Moses' thinking was much different from mine. Even though the people were completely wrong, he chose to stand with his people, upholding them. Given the same situation, what would be your reaction?

Moses' loyalty to such fickle people was almost too good to be true. Later in the same chapter Moses was again speaking with the Lord. He said, "Oh, what a great sin these people have committed! They have made themselves gods of gold. But now, please forgive their sin—but if not, then blot me out of the book you have written" (Exodus 32:31–32). Moses is saying to God, "If you destroy this people, then You'll have to destroy me too!"

Please understand that Moses was completely innocent in this situation. He was not only not involved, he was up on the mountain when the sin was committed. He was free and clear in the sight of God. Yet he chose to side with his brethren. He chose to stand in the gap on behalf of his people.

The marvelous thing in this whole story of Moses is that God honored his stand. The Lord could have easily said, "Okay, if that's the way you want it, I'll destroy all of you and start over." But He did not. Instead God honored Moses' loyalty to his brethren and ultimately withdrew His hand of judgement toward Israel.

God wants that kind of loyalty among His people. He's not interested in a half-hearted, I'll-be-loyal-when-it's-convenient attitude. The Lord wants our loyalty all of the time. How are you at remaining loyal to your brothers and sisters in Christ? To your church?

Chapter 12

*T*HE FREEDOM OF SELF-CONTROL

Poison ivy likes me. I mean it *really* likes me. If I am in close proximity to it, I generally end up with a rash. My wife, on the other hand, could probably sit down in the middle of a patch of poison ivy and have a picnic, and it would never bother her.

When I get the dreaded poison ivy rash, it itches like crazy. In my younger years I would endeavor to help alleviate the itch by—you guessed it—scratching. However, I eventually learned that scratching only helps for a short time. If you scratch the poison ivy, it will stop itching... for approximately 1.5 seconds! Then it itches more than ever. Even worse, it spreads when you scratch it. So not only does it itch more, it itches more over a bigger area. Ugh!

Today when I get poison ivy, I endeavor to leave it alone. It goes away much more quickly when I remember not to scratch it. I actually suffer less if I practice self-control.

> *When we find new freedom through Christ it is possible for us to think, "I am not bound by any rules. I can do absolutely anything I want to."*

May I be totally candid for a moment? Those first three paragraphs, although certainly relevant, were an attempt at stalling. You see, this is a chapter I really did not want to write. After all, the other areas we have discussed are much more positive. Being kind and gentle, honest and diligent—these are things that I think of as being very favorable. Self-control seems less positive to me. However, in some way the issue of self-control touches all of these others. Doing the right thing means refusing to do the wrong thing. The person of honest godly character recognizes that we need to not only display the positive aspects but also suppress the negative areas. The good things need to be brought forth, and the harmful things need to be squelched. In other words, we need to control ourselves, or practice self-control.

I recently saw a book entitled *The Freedom of Self Control*. When I read the title, I thought, "How odd. Freedom as a result of self-control? Those two ideas seem opposed to one another." The truth is, though, that they are not in opposition to each other.

When we find new freedom through Christ, the obligations of the law are removed. When this happens, it is possible for us to think, "I am not bound by any rules. I can do absolutely anything I want to." This kind of attitude would take us down a path of licentiousness and make us no different than those in the world who completely ignore the law. There is a better way: self-control.

When we practice self-control, we have the true freedom that God desires for us to have. We are no longer under the law, and we are no longer bound by the clutches of sin. Ultimate freedom comes from self-control.

> It is true that Paul told the Colossians to 'put to death, therefore, what belongs to your earthly nature' (Colossians 3:5). The Christian life has always been a walk of discipline. But it is not discipline for discipline's sake; we deny ourselves certain things because Christ has called us to something so much better.[1]

Let's be a bit more specific. We are talking about self-control or, rephrased, controlling ourselves. The word control has the connotation that we are keeping ourselves *from* something. What is it that we are to keep ourselves from?

The Bible talks about the acts of the earthly or sinful nature (Galatians 5:19-21, Colossians 3:5), and it lists such things as hatred, lust, jealousy, anger, and selfishness. Those are the kind of things over which we are to exercise self-control.

"But," you may respond, "I naturally have a quick temper. It does not take much to get me really upset." So what? If your natural tendencies disagree with God's Word, guess which one needs to change? The Word of God tells us, "A fool gives full vent to his anger, but a wise man keeps himself under control" (Proverbs 29:11). Do you want to be a fool? If not, self-control is essential.

As with nearly every character quality, we must control ourselves not just in the major events of life but also in the little things. Practicing self-control means to set those acts of the sinful nature aside as soon as they raise their ugly heads. If we entertain those things, even for a moment, they will gain an even stronger foothold in our lives. C.S. Lewis said it this way:

> Every time you make a choice you are turning the central part of you, the part of you that chooses, into something a little different from what it was before. And taking your life as a whole, with all your innumerable choices, all your life long you are slowly turning this central thing either into a heavenly creature or into a hellish creature: either into a creature that is in harmony with God, and with other creatures, and with itself, or else into one that is in a state of war and hatred with God, and with its fellow-creatures, and with itself. To be the one kind of creature is heaven: that is, it is joy and

peace and knowledge and power. To be the other means madness, horror, idiocy, rage, impotence, and eternal loneliness. Each of us at each moment is progressing to the one state or the other.[2]

Not practicing self-control ultimately will lead us to being what the Apostle Paul refers to as "slaves to sin" (Romans 6). There will be no freedom because we are enslaved to that sinful act. Self-control really is the pathway to true freedom.

I find it interesting that we frequently attribute a lack of self-control to things like tiredness or not feeling well. After verbally lashing out at someone, it is not uncommon for the offender to apologize by saying, "I didn't get enough sleep last night" or "I'm really not feeling well today." Somehow we think those rationalizations excuse our losing self-control. Consider for a moment Jesus, our example.

"But," you may respond, "I naturally have a quick temper. It does not take much to get me really upset." So what? If your natural tendencies disagree with God's Word, guess which one needs to change?

In the Garden of Gethsemane, Jesus was in such anguish that "his sweat was like drops of blood falling to the ground" (Luke 22:44). After His arrest Jesus was apparently interrogated much of the night. He may well have been awake the entire night. In the morning, when the Sanhedrin was finally finished with Him, He was brought before Pontius Pilate for more questioning, then taken to Herod, and then hauled back to Pilate. After He had been mocked, beaten, spit upon, completely humiliated and sentenced to death, Jesus was forced to carry a heavy wooden cross. He was so weak that He stumbled and could not go on. Finally, after someone else was forced to carry the burden of the cross to Golgotha, Jesus was nailed to it.

Consider this scenario. Jesus could have called a legion of angels to rescue Him. One word from Him and the entire event would have been over. Unquestionably He was tired. It is probably very safe to say that He really did not feel well. However, Jesus exhibited complete self-control throughout the entire event. How dare we suggest that we have an excuse for our lack of self-control because we got fewer hours of sleep than normal or because we have a cold or are stressed.

What about your life? Is it time for a bit more self-control in a certain area? Why not search the Scriptures about your specific area and ask God to grant a greater measure of self-control?

CHAPTER 13

THE TRICK OF TAMING THE TONGUE

If anyone considers himself religious and yet does not keep a tight rein on his tongue, he deceives himself and his religion is worthless" (James 1:26). Those are very strong words. If we don't want our religion to be "worthless," it seems imperative that we understand what it means to keep a tight rein on our tongue.

In her book titled *A Mother's Touch*, Elise Arndt describes what she did when she caught her children speaking harshly or negatively toward one another.

> The way we have learned to handle this particular problem in our home is by counteracting every bad word with a good one. We base this on Philippians 4:8: "Finally, brethren, whatever is true, whatever is honorable, whatever is right, whatever is pure, whatever is lovely, whatever is of good repute, if there is any excellence, and if anything worthy of praise, let your mind dwell on these things." When a derogatory word is said about another person I make the person who said it counteract it by saying something especially nice about that one.[1]

What would happen if we made this a practice in the church?! Every time someone in the Church makes a negative comment about another person, we should immediately ask them to say something nice about that person. I would be willing to wager that we could wipe out negative comments within one month.

The Bible is very clear about how we are to talk about one another. "Brothers, do not slander one another. Anyone who speaks against his brother or judges him speaks against the law and judges it. When you judge the law, you are not keeping it, but sitting in judgement on it" (James 4:11). If we are busy judging others, we are missing God's plan for *our* lives.

Some time ago I read an interesting fictional book entitled *The Portal*. In it two friends, Nathan and Denise, are taken from our world to a land called Fayrah, in another dimension. There are physical differences between Fayrah and our world, but the major difference is that there no one criticizes anyone else. Everyone speaks words of encouragement to each other.

Once there, Nathan and Denise become separated, and he begins to say bad things about her. Each time he does, a horrendous pain shoots through Denise's head and body. One of the inhabitants of Fayrah, Aristophenix, tells Denise that the pain must be because Nathan is saying bad things about her. He explains in his poetic talking style:

> Your words can cut
> and force others to bleed,
> 'cause they're spoken
>   from mouths
> which have been Image-
>   Breathed.

"If anyone considers himself religious and yet does not keep a tight rein on his tongue, he deceives himself and his religion is worthless" (James 1:26).

As the reality of what Aristophenix is saying dawns on her, Denise responds, "You mean Nathan is doing all this to me with his mouth? This is all happening because of what he is saying?"

Her companions nod.

"Great authority have Upside Downers [earthlings]. Powerful very, their words of blessing or cursing."[2]

These thoughts echo the words of Solomon. "The mouth of the righteous is a fountain of life" (Proverbs 10:11). We should choose our words carefully in order to bring life, not pain and death.

> *A normal form of verbal interaction in our society is put-downs— cutting remarks designed to destroy one another, or, at least, to bring others down a notch or two. We Christians should be doing the opposite.*

"Reckless words pierce like a sword, but the tongue of the wise brings healing" (Proverbs 12:18). Our words can actually help bring healing and restoration.

"The tongue that brings healing is a tree of life, but a deceitful tongue crushes the spirit" (Proverbs 15:4). It is imperative to use our tongues correctly in order to avoid crushing anyone's spirit with our words.

"The tongue has the power of life and death" (Proverbs 18:21). *Life and death!*

Some time ago I encountered the pastor of a nearby church at the post office. I have ministered at his church on several occasions, and he and I know one another very well. He mentioned that the week prior he had been talking with some believers from another church. During the course of the conversation one of them began to share some very destructive rumors he had heard about my pastor. My friend immediately stopped the man and told him that the rumors were not true and that he would do well to check out rumors before spreading them any further. This should be essential advice for the Church. "He who covers over an offense promotes love, but whoever repeats the matter separates close friends" (Proverbs 17:9).

Scripture does not pull any punches when addressing the issue of gossip. It is not acceptable. Period. One cannot honestly read the Bible and think that it is permissible to gossip.

Earlier we looked at Psalm 15, one of the shortest chapters in the Bible. It contains only six verses. Verse one asks the question, "LORD, who may dwell in your sanctuary? Who may live on your holy hill?" In our modern vernacular we might phrase it, "Who can come before God?" The rest of the psalm gives character traits of those the Lord deems acceptable to come before Him. Verse three describes such a person as one who "has no slander on his tongue, who does his neighbor no wrong and casts no slur on his fellowman." God does not want us slandering or casting a slur on our brothers and sisters in the Lord.

Scripture is also very clear on the proper way to handle the situation if we believe someone has sinned against us:

> If your brother sins against you, go and show him his fault, just between the two of you. If he listens to you, you have won your brother over. But if he will not listen, take one or two others along, so that "every matter may be established by the testimony of two or three witnesses." If he refuses to listen to them, tell it to the church; and if he

refuses to listen even to the church, treat him as
you would a pagan or a tax collector (Matthew
18:15–17).

Spreading rumors is never acceptable. In the verses
above Jesus very plainly spells out the appropriate action to
take when we believe we have been wronged. Do not tell
everyone else about it first. Go to the person and confront
him. If that does not work, then take two or three others
with you the next time. However, you must still be talking
to the person, not spreading rumors about him. Anyone
unwilling to take these simple steps has absolutely no business spreading stories, true or untrue, about another person.

We must be very careful with our words. "With the
tongue we praise our Lord and Father, and with it we curse
men, who have been made in God's likeness. Out of the
same mouth come praising and cursing. My brothers, this
should not be" (James 3:9–10).

One day Jesus told His followers, "You have heard that
it was said to the people long ago, 'Do not murder, and anyone who murders will be subject to judgment.' But I tell you
that anyone who is angry with his brother will be subject to
judgment. Again, anyone who says to his brother, 'Raca,' is
answerable to the Sanhedrin. But anyone who says, 'You
fool!' will be in danger of the fire of hell" (Matthew
5:21–22).

The word "raca" (*rhak-ah´*) literally means "empty
head." Today our equivalent of this word would be "air-
head." Jesus is telling the people that simply calling one
another names puts them in danger of judgment!

A normal form of verbal interaction in our society is
put-downs—cutting remarks designed to destroy one

another, or at least to bring others down a notch or two. The truth is that we Christians should be doing the opposite. We have enough detractors in the world. We should use our words to build one another up. "Do not let any unwholesome talk come out of your mouths, but only what is helpful for building others up according to their needs, that it may benefit those who listen" (Ephesians 4:29).

The apostle James tells us: "When we put bits into the mouths of horses to make them obey us, we can turn the whole animal. Or take ships as an example. Although they are so large and are driven by strong winds, they are steered by a very small rudder wherever the pilot wants to go" (James 3:3–4). Having given us these examples from everyday life, he then goes on to reinforce how powerful our words can be.

How about you? Is your tongue under control? Are there moments when you say things about others that you clearly should not have said? Part of the honest display of godly character in our lives is controlling our words.

CHAPTER 14

THE GOAL OF
GRATEFULNESS

Some years ago I had the opportunity to minister in Eastern Europe. While in Poland I was consistently amazed by the thankfulness of the people. By American standards most of the people in that nation lived in poverty. (Honestly, I think they were fine. We just have an overinflated idea of what "normal" is in America.) Even in the midst of their deprivation, however, their gratefulness was overwhelming.

I remember being in a worship service early in the trip. Later in the service I would preach, but prior to that the people were singing praises to God. At one point the singing came to an end but the musicians continued to play quietly in the background. Suddenly a man from the congregation spoke aloud. Then another. Then a woman. Others followed. Since I am not even mildly fluent in Polish, I asked our interpreter what they were saying. As she interpreted each person's monologue, I found

> *I stood there in the midst of such honest gratefulness and wept. I wondered if people in our country—even in the midst of our overwhelming affluence—could find as many things for which they could thank God.*

that they were talking with God. Each was thanking the Lord for blessings received. I certainly do not recall everything for which they thanked God that evening, but I do remember being astounded that they could come up with so many things for which to be thankful: their homes, their families, their church, the American missionaries being there, their friends, some seemingly insignificant blessing received that day, answered prayers...on and on they prayed, thanking God one after another.

I stood there in the midst of such honest gratefulness and wept. I wondered if people in our country—even in the midst of our overwhelming affluence—could find as many things for which they could thank God if given the opportunity. I repented for my own lack of thankfulness and prayed that I would always have a thankful heart.

George Herbert, a seventeenth-century Anglican poet, said, "You have given so much to me. Give me one thing more—a grateful heart."[1] We all certainly need that.

Some time ago my wife shared a story with me about a mother who was endeavoring to teach her children to be grateful. The kids were apparently having great struggles with doing anything but complaining. This mom had her children make a list of things for which they were grateful. The next day each child was permitted to use only the things on their list. If they hadn't put toys on the list, they couldn't play with them. If they forgot clothes, they stayed in their pajamas. If they omitted food, they missed breakfast. It was not long before they had to abort the exercise, since they had left so many things off their lists. When they were given another chance to make their lists, they were much more grateful.

Not being grateful is certainly not a modern-day American phenomenon. Jesus encountered the same heart attitude during His earthly ministry.

> Now on His way to Jerusalem, Jesus traveled along the border between Samaria and Galilee. As he was going into a village, ten men who had leprosy met him. They stood at a distance and called

out in a loud voice, "Jesus, Master, have pity on us!"

When He saw them, He said, "Go, show yourselves to the priests." And as they went, they were cleansed.

One of them, when he saw he was healed, came back, praising God in a loud voice. He threw himself at Jesus' feet and thanked Him—and he was a Samaritan.

Jesus asked, "Were not all ten cleansed? Where are the other nine? Was no one found to return and give praise to God except this foreigner?" (Luke 17:11-18)

Jesus seems to be astonished by the lack of gratefulness. "Were not all ten cleansed? Where are the other nine?" Jesus was not on some kind of ego trip, desiring to be acknowledged to somehow boost His self-esteem. As always, Jesus was thinking about *them*. He was concerned about *their* hearts. He did not want them to take a blessing from God for granted.

The apostle Paul wrote much about being grateful. Numerous times in his writings, Paul exclaimed, "Thanks be to God" (Romans 6:17; 7:25; 1 Corinthians 15:57; 2 Corinthians 2:14; 9:15). He even told us that we should be "always giving thanks" (Ephesians 5:20) and that we should "give thanks in all circumstances" (1 Thessalonians 5:18). "Always" and "in all circumstances" are pretty lofty goals for which we should aim.

Several years ago I heard a man speaking about the importance of the Word of God. During his teaching he shared this passage: "Seven times a day I praise you for your righteous laws" (Psalm 119:164). His point from this verse is that we need to give thanks and praise to God for His Word. As I listened, my thought process went something like this: "Yes, that's right. However, do we praise God seven times a day for anything? And if we did would it make a difference in our lives?"

I have a very vivid imagination. Consequently, in thinking about this praising-God-seven- times-a-day passage, I began to wonder how we could make this a reality. Perhaps we could do it like this:

Jesus seems to be astonished by the lack of gratefulness: "Were not all ten cleansed? Where are the other nine?"

1. First thing in the morning
2. Right after breakfast
3. Mid-morning
4. Right after lunch
5. Mid-afternoon
6. Right after supper
7. Before bedtime

What do you suppose would happen if we actually stopped for just a few minutes at each one of those times and gave thanks and praise to God? I'm not even referring to just thanking Him for His Word. You can pick the topic. Just give Him thanks and praise. Doing something like that would certainly begin to stir a heart of thankfulness within us.

In the Old Testament, David's heart was so full of thankfulness to God that he concluded one of his most moving psalms, "O LORD my God, I will give you thanks forever" (Psalm 30:12). David was not even satisfied to be grateful here and now. He vowed to thank God forever.

We need to cultivate that heart of thankfulness in our own lives. We certainly don't want to be like the nine lepers who never thanked Jesus for their healing. Our goal should be to be grateful to Him always and in all circumstances—even forever.

Are you grateful to God for the blessings in your life? Do you regularly voice that thankfulness? Godly character is displayed in many different ways, but an attitude of gratitude—thanking the Lord for His manifold blessings—clearly shows God is at work in us.

CHAPTER 15

ℐHE SATISFACTION OF SERVANTHOOD

I n our time and culture the concept of being a servant seems alien to us. Most of us don't even know someone who makes a living as a servant. That type of job is certainly out of the ordinary in our society.

In Jesus' day people understood the idea of servants. People who were servants by vocation were commonplace. However, even though they apparently understood servanthood much better than we do, Jesus' statement that to become the greatest you must become "the servant of all" (Mark 9:35) called for quite a radical shift in thinking.

Jesus not only spoke of servanthood. He even demonstrated the idea. His washing of His disciples' feet clearly had a very strong impact on His followers.

> Jesus knew that the Father had put all things under his power, and that he had come from God and was returning to God; so he got up from the meal, took off his outer clothing, and wrapped a towel around his waist. After that, he poured water into a basin and began to wash his disciples' feet, drying them with the towel that was wrapped around him (John 13:3–5).

We don't think like that in our culture. We want accolades. We want to be noticed. We want people to think we're great.

Do you remember the time when the mother of James and John asked Jesus if her sons could sit on either side of Jesus when He came into His kingdom? James and John were right there assuring Jesus they also thought this was a really good idea. Later the other disciples found out. "When the ten heard about this, they were indignant with the two brothers" (Matthew 20:24).

Why were the others indignant? There is only one logical answer to that question. They wanted those places. They each wanted the highest positions. This must have been an ongoing problem among the disciples because Jesus heard them arguing another time. "He asked them, 'What were you arguing about on the road?' But they kept quiet because on the way they had argued about who was the greatest" (Mark 9:33–34). It was at this point that Jesus told them, "If anyone wants to be first, he must be the very last, and the servant of all" (vs. 35).

Our attitude is, "Me, be a servant?! No thanks." However, Jesus clearly told us that if we indeed want to be great then we must become servants. "Whoever wants to become great among you must be your servant, and whoever wants to be first must be your slave" (Matthew 20:26–27).

The word "slave" in this verse literally means "bond-slave." In that society it was not uncommon for someone to be enslaved for a certain period of time in order to work off a debt. Occasionally, when the time was over, a person who had been treated extremely

> *Because May was willing to become a bond-slave to an abandoned child, one that our society would label as "worthless," Leslie was able to offer hope and happiness to thousands of people.*

well by his master realized that this lifestyle was better than what he had waiting for him when he regained his freedom. When this happened, the person could willingly ask to become a bond-slave. This meant that he was choosing to give up his freedom for the rest of his life and become a slave to this kind master. There was no coercion involved. It was completely voluntary. In fact, to demonstrate his commitment to his master, the slave would allow the master to pierce his ear (usually with a rather primitive instrument like an awl) and place a small, plain gold hoop earring in his ear. Whenever someone wore such an earring, it was a sign to everyone that this was a bond-slave—a person who had willingly given up their freedom to serve someone else.

Some time ago I read an article about a woman named May Lemke. When she was fifty-two years old and had already raised five children of her own, May agreed to take in a six-month-old infant named Leslie who had been abandoned by his parents. Mentally retarded and without eyes, Leslie also had cerebral palsy and was totally unresponsive to sound or touch.

May spent the next eighteen years loving Leslie and endeavoring to teach him the simple tasks of life. Nothing was second nature to Leslie. The things we take for granted, like eating and walking, took him many years to learn. During this time May consistently prayed over Leslie, asking God to show her how to help him develop.

One day she noticed Leslie "pluck" a taut string around a package. Based on this action, she began to fill their house with music. She consistently had music playing during their waking hours. May and her husband, Joe, even bought an old upright piano. She repeatedly pushed Leslie's fingers against the keys to show him that he could make sounds with his fingers. During all of this Leslie remained totally indifferent.

Then it happened. One morning at 3 a.m. May was awakened by the musical strains of Tchaikovsky's Piano Concerto No. 1. She shook Joe and asked if he had left the radio on.

"No," he said.

May went immediately to Leslie's room. She found him sitting at the piano, smiling. He had never gotten out of bed on his own before. He had never seated himself at the piano. He had never voluntarily or deliberately struck the keys with his fingers. Now he was playing a concerto—with deftness and confidence.

From that point Leslie's musical abilities developed. He went on to play piano at churches, civic clubs, schools, colleges, county fairs, and finally network television. Because May was willing to become a bond-slave to an abandoned child,

> *I imagine Jesus helped collect firewood for their cold evenings in the countryside. With His carpentry skills, He most likely repaired more than one door or chair in a home where He stayed.*

one that our society would label as "worthless," Leslie was able to offer hope and happiness to thousands of people.

Jesus told His followers, "The Son of Man did not come to be served, but to serve" (Matthew 20:28). If we understand this statement, and if we understand that Jesus never embellished the truth, then it appears obvious that Jesus did not sit around while others waited on Him hand and foot. Certainly there were times when He exercised His leadership. However, Jesus clearly could not have honestly made this statement about not coming to be served if he had consistently sat around like a potentate expecting others to jump at His every whim. I imagine Jesus helped collect firewood for their cold evenings in the countryside. I picture Him offering to carry water. With His carpentry skills, He most likely repaired more than one door or chair in a home where He stayed.

What about you? Do you offer to help with the dishes? Do you open the door for a stranger (or maybe for someone close to you)? Are the menial tasks of life beneath you? Are you really a servant?

Jesus summarized the servant attitude we should have when He shared these words:

> Suppose one of you had a servant plowing or looking after the sheep. Would he say to the servant when he comes in from the field, "Come along now and sit down to eat"? Would he not rather say, "Prepare my supper, get yourself ready and wait on me while I eat and drink; after that you may eat and drink"? Would he thank the servant because he did what he was told to do? So you also, when you have done everything you were told to do, should say, "We are unworthy servants; we have only done our duty" (Luke 17:7–10).

Quite some time ago I attended a large Christian conference. Toward the end of the conference there was an appreciation ceremony to honor those who had done such a marvelous job of taking care of all the details of the event. Especially honored were the husband and wife who had tirelessly spearheaded the coordination of all the volunteers necessary for the conference. Several people shared what a tremendous job this couple had done. Finally, when it was time for them to respond, they stood. The wife said nothing and the husband said just four words: "It was our pleasure." Then they sat down. There was not even a hint of, "Look at us. Didn't we do a great job?" Their servant hearts shone through clearly.

In Matthew 25 Jesus told the parable of the talents. Toward the end of the story, the master says to those who were faithful, "Well done, good and faithful servant!" (Matthew 25:21, 23). This story was meant to parallel the kingdom of God. The ending represents the great last day when we meet the Lord face to face. It is my personal conviction that, as long as we are part of His kingdom, we will all hear those words, "Well done, good and faithful servant." (Please realize that it has very little to do with us but everything to do with God's faithfulness.) But, when we hear those words, what will our reaction be? "Oh yeah, God, remember the time I led those four kids to salvation at vacation Bible school?" At that point, who cares?!

When I look into my Savior's eyes and He tells me, "Well done, good and faithful servant," the only possible response will be to look at Him through tear-filled eyes and say, "Lord, thank You so much for the opportunity just to serve You!" That should be our attitude here and now also. We're really no one special, just unworthy servants doing our duty. Are you comfortable and active serving others? Do you need to allow God to work in your heart an attitude that counts it a privilege to serve?

CHAPTER 16

THE HONOR OF HUMILITY

My family and I recently visited Appomattox, Virginia, the site of the surrender ending the Civil War. I found one of the presentations there to be particularly enlightening. After General Lee had signed the surrender, there was much excitement among the Union troops. Their commander, General Grant, quickly issued an order that there should be no exuberant displays of triumph. Both armies were once again part of a united nation, and there should be no gloating over their brothers' loss. Although Grant had clearly beaten Lee and shown superiority in both manpower and tactical maneuvering, Grant refused to flaunt his victory. He displayed much humility, even in a situation where he could easily have become haughty.

"Humble yourselves, therefore, under God's mighty hand, that he may lift you up in due time" (1 Peter 5:6). Let's be candid. Humility is a very rare commodity in our culture. I looked up antonyms to "humble" in a thesaurus. I found words like arrogant, defiant, haughty, overbearing and pompous. Unfortunately all of those things are far more common in our culture than true humility.

> *I looked up antonyms to "humble" in a thesaurus. I found words like arrogant, defiant, haughty, overbearing and pompous.*

As usual, the kingdom of God is in direct opposition to the ways of the world. Scripture is clear on this issue: "All of you, clothe yourselves with humility toward one another, because 'God opposes the proud but gives grace to the humble'" (1 Peter 5:5). "All of you" doesn't seem to leave any loopholes for those who do not have a natural tendency toward being humble. It means that even if we are uncomfortable with being humble, we should do it anyway.

In the last half of this verse Peter even gives us a practical reason for being humble: "because 'God opposes the proud but gives grace to the humble.'" Do you want to be in opposition to God? Me neither. I will gladly receive all the grace available to me, though, so I need to be humble.

The letter to the Philippians gives us further understanding of humility: "In humility consider others better than yourselves" (Philippians 2:3). Considering others as being better than ourselves is true humility. Unfortunately, most of us find this idea extremely foreign—even contrary—to our way of thinking. "Me?! Consider someone else better than myself?! You've got to be kidding!" If you're a Christian, you probably would not actually say those words, but God looks at the heart. It is not adequate to be intellectually astute enough to repress the expression of our lack of humility. Real humility begins on the inside.

> Your attitude should be the same as that of Christ Jesus: Who, being in very nature God, did not consider equality with God something to be grasped, but made himself nothing, taking the very nature of a servant, being made in human likeness. And being found in appearance as a man, he humbled himself and became obedient to death—even death on a cross! (Philippians 2:5–8).

Part of Jesus' mission here on earth was to be an example for us. Interestingly, at every juncture He seems to have chosen what we would consider to be the wrong road. The Creator chose to become the creature. In becoming a creature, He could have chosen to be a man. Instead He became a baby. When He grew up He could have become a king.

Instead He became a servant. Then He chose to die a miserable death to pay for the sins of His creation. From our normal human perspective, each step seems to be in the wrong direction.

However, the final outcome of taking those "wrong" roads was far greater than we could have imagined. "Therefore God exalted him to the highest place and gave him the name that is above every name, that at the name of Jesus every knee should bow, in heaven and on earth and under the earth, and every tongue confess that Jesus Christ is Lord, to the glory of God the Father" (Philippians 2:9–11). Jesus chose to be humble. Therefore God exalted Him.

> *The important message for us is that we do not have to go through God's humbling process. We can choose to be humble.*

For the Christian, humility is not just an option. It is mandatory. We do, however, have a choice as to *how* we will be humble. We can be humble voluntarily, or God will humble us. Either option can be very effective. My experience, though, has been that the first is a much easier path. God's humbling process can sometimes be extremely painful.

In the Old Testament, Jacob's son Joseph was a visionary destined for greatness (read his entire story in Genesis 37–50). Unfortunately Joseph seems to have lacked humility. When God began to unveil His plan for Joseph through a series of dreams, Joseph arrogantly shared those dreams with his family. After the first dream he had the nerve to let his brothers know that they someday would be bowing down to him. Their reaction to the first incident should have been adequate to create at least a bit of humility in Joseph. Unfortunately Joseph did not seem to catch on. The next dream he shared was even stronger, and this time he even alienated his father, who loved Joseph more than he loved the others.

Do you see the dilemma? God had destined Joseph for great things but Joseph had little humility. Although God gave him the opportunity, Joseph did not humble himself. There was only one option left—God's humbling process.*

Joseph's brothers sold him into slavery. He was taken from his homeland to a neighboring country where he worked hard and developed into an excellent steward of his master's property. It was evident that the Lord was with him in all he did. Unfortunately, it appears from the story that God had a more thorough humbling process in mind for Joseph. Through no fault of his own Joseph ended up in prison. Only as the result of hard work, diligence, and the obvious intervention of God, was he exonerated.

Finally, after several years and numerous extremely trying situations, the Lord's humbling process was over. The good news is that the process was obviously a success. When Joseph's dreams about his brothers bowing before

---

*Please understand that Scripture does not directly state that Joseph went through these trials to humble him. Also understand that I am not suggesting that this was the only reason he went through the things he did. However, the final outcome of the sequence of events in his life certainly appears to be a humility that was lacking earlier.

him were finally fulfilled, there is no hint of arrogance on the part of Joseph. In fact, no longer the haughty little brother, Joseph wept openly and embraced his brothers. God's humbling process was effective.

The important message for us is that we do not have to go through God's humbling process. We can choose to be humble. However, it is not just a bit of humility that the Lord desires. Paul said, "Be completely humble" (Ephesians 4:2). Just a little humbleness is not acceptable. We need to be *completely* humble. If we choose to be humble, we can avoid the humbling process. On the other hand we can be proud and haughty, considering ourselves as better than others. In that case, like it or not, God will implement a process for humbling us. Remember, "God opposes the proud but gives grace to the humble" (1 Peter 5:5).

So, are you *completely* humble? Are there areas and attitudes of arrogance that need to be eliminated? You can either face them now and humble yourself in God's grace, or you can wait and let the Lord humble you through difficult times.

CHAPTER 17

THE IMPORTANCE OF EXCELLENCE

Some time ago I had the opportunity to visit a fascinating exhibit at the St. Louis Zoo. In it there were numerous displays of "exotic" animals from around the world. Unfortunately, all through the exhibit there were blatant as well as subtle references to evolution. As I walked through the display two feelings came over me. The first was pity for the learned scientists who believe that all of these things came into being simply by chance. The second was an overwhelming awe of the God of creation Who made all of these creatures. His creativity is limitless. The variety in those creatures was so great that it seems to take more "faith" to believe that they were an accident than to believe in a God Who created them.

God apparently held nothing back when He created the earth on which we live. Why, after all, did the Lord make the creatures in the ocean depths which no human would even discover until this century? Why did He make each animal unique? Why so many different kinds? Would not just a few dozen have been sufficient? It seems apparent that God chose to make creation not just a half-hearted effort but the absolute best it could be. This attitude was manifest in Jesus also. When the people witnessed His healing ministry, they responded, "He has done everything well" (Mark 7:37).

We in the church need to grasp the concept of excellence more fully. Over the past several years I have frequently had the opportunity to interact with those involved in various ministries in churches. There have been more times than I care to remember when I have encountered someone doing a half-hearted job with the attitude of, "It's good enough for church." This attitude is totally opposite from God's perspective.

God's Word tells us, "One who is slack in his work is brother to one who destroys" (Proverbs 18:9). From the Lord's perspective not doing your best is akin to being a destroyer. Clearly God is not interested in a half-hearted effort but in excellence.

> In the second century, Christian apologist Justin Martyr grew up over the hill from Galilee.

Interestingly, he notes that the plows made by Joseph and Jesus were still being used widely in his day. How intriguing to think of Jesus' plows...to wonder what it was that made His plows and yokes last and stand out.[1]

Wooden plows that were used regularly and lasted more than 100 years? This was not merely "acceptable" craftsmanship. The work of Joseph and Jesus was apparently outstanding. The reality is that they could have cut some corners and not done such a quality job. After all, if the plows lasted just thirty years, surely the purchaser would have been satisfied. There certainly could not be recourse for any type of reimbursement if a regularly-used plow made it through fifty years of plowing. Why expend so much effort to make plows that would last so amazingly long? "Whatever you do, work at it with all your heart, as working for the Lord, not for men" (Colossians 3:23).

> *Wooden plows that were used regularly and lasted more than 100 years? This was not merely "acceptable" craftsmanship.*

Author and teacher Os Guiness, in his book *The Call*, said, "Instead of doing things because of their intrinsic importance—their value in themselves—we do things for instrumental reasons—their value for our self-expression, our fulfilment, our profit, and our publicity."[2] Unfortunately, he's right. We are too often more self-motivated than God-motivated. "What's in it for me?" is a common thought. Instead our attitude should be, "What's the right thing to do?" and "How can I glorify the Lord in this?"

If we really want to follow the Lord, then we have no choice but to desire and pursue excellence. The standard of excellence is simply a part of the nature of the God Whom we serve. We need to strike the death blow to mediocrity within the church. If we can grasp and implement this attitude in our lives, we will see the blessing of God poured out upon us to maintain it.

Praying toward that end is the main key. Throughout Scripture God repeatedly caused His people to stand out from the crowd. "To these four young men [Shadrach, Meshach, Abednego, and Daniel] God gave knowledge and understanding of all kinds of literature and learning. And Daniel could understand visions and dreams of all kinds.... In every matter of wisdom and understanding about which the king questioned them, he found them ten times better than all the magicians and enchanters in his whole kingdom" (Daniel 1:17, 20). God is no respecter of persons. What He did for Shadrach, Meshach, Abednego, and Daniel, He can do for us if we will ask Him.

It has been said that excellence speaks a language all its own. Excellence certainly makes a much stronger statement than mediocrity. We must pursue excellence with all our might.

One key point here is how we measure excellence. God's Word is the final, true measuring rod. Walking in grace, however, we need to be careful not to compare ourselves with other people and/or other people's ideas. "Each one should test his own actions. Then he can take pride in himself, without comparing himself to somebody else" (Galatians 6:4). If we are stretching ourselves to strive for *more* excellence, we are headed in the right direction.

We should have the attitude of, "Regardless of what others think, regardless of what it costs me, I will pursue godly excellence, even as my Creator has pursued it." If we will pursue this attitude of excellence in all that we do, God will be honored and, in return, honor our efforts.

What about your life? Are there areas where you settle for second-best because it's "for church"? Do you now recognize the necessity of striving toward excellence in all areas of your life?

$\mathcal{I}$T IS GOD'S WORK

In his book *The Jesus I Never Knew*, Philip Yancey shared this poignant story:

> I remember vividly a meeting with the editors
> of *Pravda*, formerly the official mouthpiece of the
> Communist Party. *Pravda* as much as any institu-
> tion had slavishly served the Communist 'church.'

Now, though, *Pravda's* circulation was falling dramatically (from eleven million to 700,000) in concert with communism's fall from grace. The editors of *Pravda* seemed earnest, sincere, searching—and shaken to the core. So shaken that they were now asking advice from emissaries of a religion their founder had scorned as 'the opiate of the people.'

The editors remarked wistfully that Christianity and communism have many of the same ideals: equality, sharing, justice, and racial harmony. Yet they had to admit the Marxist pursuit of that vision had produced the worst nightmares the world has ever seen. Why?

"We don't know how to motivate people to show compassion," said the editor-in-chief. "We tried raising money for the children of Chernobyl, but the average Russian citizen would rather spend his money on drink. How do you reform and motivate people? How do you get them to be good?"

Seventy-four years of communism had proved beyond all doubt that goodness could not be legislated from the Kremlin and enforced at the point of a gun. In a heavy irony, attempts to compel morality tend to produce defiant subjects and tyrannical rulers who lose their moral core. I came away from Russia with the strong sense that we Christians would do well to relearn the basic lesson... Goodness cannot be imposed externally... it must grow internally..."[1]

In the following four chapters I will endeavor to lay a foundation that is absolutely vital to the formation of godly character in our lives. Without a clear understanding of these principles, the previous chapters that describe specific godly characteristics will ultimately cause us to be manufacturing soiled scraps of cloth. "All our righteous acts are like filthy rags" (Isaiah 64:6).

In his book *A Godward Life*, John Piper states:

> I need help. Always. In everything. I am simply kidding myself if I think I can move an inch without God's help. For God gives to all "life and breath and all things" (Acts 17:25). I need it for the sake of my own weak faith. I need it to inflame the smoldering wick of my zeal. I need it for empowering in evangelism. I need it for authentic worship. I need it for courage in righteous living. I need it to transform my teenagers into God-centered, humble, respectful young people. I need it so I can minister hope and joy and boldness to our missionaries. I need it for guidance in future planning. I need it for a thousand other demands and stresses and joyful possibilities.[2]

Jesus clearly told us, "Apart from me you can do nothing" (John 15:5b). Ultimately, the displaying of godly character in our lives must be seen as God's work in us. "For it is God who works in you to will and to act according to his good purpose" (Philippians 2:13). God gives us both the desire ("to will") and the ability ("to act") to do what He wants us to do. It is not so much a matter of us gritting our teeth and trying harder to be more godly, but trusting in His grace at work in us. Hard to believe? Let's see what Scripture has to say.

"But the fruit of the Spirit is love, joy, peace, patience, kindness, goodness, faithfulness, gentleness and self-control" (Galatians 5:22-23a). It is easy to read this verse and miss the real meaning. The Bible refers to children as the "fruit of the womb." Where do children originate? In the womb. Apples originate on apple trees. Fruit must come from whatever would bear that type of fruit. Similarly, these great character qualities (love, joy, peace, patience, etc.) are referred to as "the fruit *of the Spirit.*" They do not come from trying to make them occur. Instead they are produced by the Holy Spirit (their origin) at work in us. If the Holy Spirit is at work in a person's life then that person will bear the fruit of the Spirit. Without the Holy Spirit no amount of striving or trying harder can manufacture the real thing.

It is interesting to note that in Scripture everything God requires of us He also gives us. He is our sole source of supply. I remember Dr. Judson Cornwall talking about this concept a number of years ago. He mentioned that when his children were younger, they would drop "lightly veiled hints" about needing to earn some money. Although these times were near his birthday and Father's Day, he was expected not to notice the connection. He was, in essence, supplying himself with his own presents because he was his children's only source of supply.

The same is true for God's interaction with us. Apart from the Lord, we can do nothing. He is our total source of supply. "His divine power has given us *everything* we need for life and godliness through our knowledge of him who called us by his own glory and goodness" (2 Peter 1:3, author's emphasis). Please note that this verse does not say that we have been given "some things" or even "almost everything" we need for godliness. "Everything" means everything. It is not our own strength but *God* who has given us all we need for godliness.

The very next verse adds a bit more understanding to this text. "He has given us his very great and precious promises, *so that through them* you may participate in the divine nature and escape the corruption in the world caused by evil desires" (vs. 4, author's emphasis). Peter is clearly telling us here that it is through the promises of God that we "participate in the divine nature and escape the corruption in the world caused by evil desires." It is not by trying harder that we become more godly. It is by trusting His promises. God works through the promises of His Word to produce change in us.

> *"Goodness cannot be imposed externally... it must grow internally ..."*

These are not isolated Scriptures. The Bible is clear that the Lord Himself is the One who causes us to become more like Him. "And God is able to make all grace abound to you, so that in all things at all times, having all that you need, you will abound in every good work" (2 Corinthians 9:8). Clearly it is God's grace, not our own self-will, that causes us to "abound in every good work."

"May the God of peace...equip you with everything good for doing his will, and may he work in us what is pleasing to him, through Jesus Christ" (Hebrews 13:20–21). Who is going to work in us what is "pleasing to him"? God is.

Paul the apostle prays for the church at Thessalonica in his first letter to them: "May *the Lord* make your love increase and overflow for each other and for everyone else, just as ours does for you. May *he* strengthen your hearts so that you will be blameless and holy in the presence of our God and Father when our Lord Jesus comes with all his holy ones" (1 Thessalonians 3:12–13, author's emphasis). Who was Paul petitioning for increased love and strengthened hearts? It was God who would work in them to accomplish His purposes.

> *If satan can get us to question our relationship with God, he has effectively unplugged us from the only power source that will ever really make a difference in our lives.*

"To this end I labor, struggling with all his energy, which so powerfully works in me" (Colossians 1:29). Paul was not struggling with his own energy, but God's. It was the Lord's strength that was working powerfully in Paul.

"Being confident of this, that he who began a good work in you will carry it on to completion until the day of Christ Jesus" (Philippians 1:6). We are confident in Him because of His promises.

"Let us hold unswervingly to the hope we profess, for he who promised is faithful" (Hebrews 10:23). Our hope is not that we can somehow make ourselves better people by our own strength. When we do that, we are merely producing the same filthy rags which Isaiah condemned. It is God's power at work in us that brings changes.

Do you recall the time Jesus was being tempted by Satan in the wilderness? When we look at that section of Scripture, we often see the first temptation as Satan suggesting Jesus turn stones into bread. Although this was a wise temptation (Jesus had been fasting for 40 days and was undoubtedly hungry), it was not the first.

The first temptation is found in Satan's first seven words: "If you are the Son of God" (Matthew 4:3). He was questioning Jesus' relationship with the Father. And he does the same thing to you and me. "*You*, a child of God?! After what you did today?! Not a chance!" Or, "You're not *really* a Christian! Just take a look at your life!" How many times have you heard those words (or something similar) questioning your relationship with your heavenly Father? It is exactly the same tactic Satan used on Jesus. The father of lies continues to use the same strategy on us for one simple reason: he knows that if he can get us to question our relationship with God, he has effectively unplugged us from the only power source that will ever really make a difference in our lives.

This entire concept is very different from our society's normal way of thinking. Many people have the idea that in order to be more godly, we as Christians must work harder. We must strive to become more like Jesus. This line of thinking suggests that if we will simply put forth the necessary effort the final result will eventually be Christ-likeness. Although this sounds pious enough, the concept misses our fundamental principle. The formation of godly character in our lives must be seen as a work of God.

Years ago, when my children were much younger, they were unable to write on their own. When they would color a picture for Mommy I would help them sign it. I would take the child's hand in mine and help him form the letters. He was signing the picture but only because I was assisting. Without my aid there would have been no real signature. Similarly God uses our efforts, but it is He alone who ultimately does the real work, and He alone should get the glory for it.

Steve Fry, known more for his music ministry than his teaching, said, "Mature behavior comes not so much from our struggle to be good as it does from our exhilarating response to God's calling. God didn't just save us; He united our spirits to His and walked inside our body."[3]

"For it is by grace you have been saved, through *faith— and this not from yourselves, it is the gift of God*—not by works, so that no one can boast" (Ephesians 2:8–9, author's emphasis). Even the very faith by which we are saved is a gift from God! In the final analysis, all that we have and all that we will ever become are gifts from God. Even if we become so sanctified that people immediately recognize the image of Jesus in us, it will not be from our own efforts. "For who makes you different from anyone else? What do you have that you did not receive? And if you did receive it, why do you boast as though you did not?" (1 Corinthians 4:7). John Ortberg said it this way:

> "The wind blows where it chooses," Jesus said, "and you hear the sound of it, but you do not know where it comes from or where it goes. So it is with everyone who is born of the Spirit."
>
> Consider the difference between piloting a motorboat or a sailboat. We can run a motorboat all by ourselves. We can fill the tank and start the engine. We are in control. But a sailboat is a

different story. We can hoist the sails and steer the rudder, but we are utterly dependent on the wind. The wind does the work. If the wind doesn't blow—and sometimes it doesn't—we sit still in the water no matter how frantic we act. Our task is to do whatever enables us to catch the wind.

Spiritual transformation is that way. We may be aggressively pursuing it, but we cannot turn it on and off. We can open ourselves to transformation through certain practices, but we cannot engineer it. We can take no credit for it.[4]

If we attain anything on our own, who gets the credit for it? We do, of course. More importantly, if we take the glory for our diligent efforts of godly character development in our lives, Who (that capital "W" is a clue) does *not* get the glory? "I am the LORD; that is My name! I will not give My glory to another or My praise to idols" (Isaiah 42:8). God should get all the credit. Why? Because He is ultimately the one working His good in us.

CHAPTER 19

GRACE MAKES ALL THE DIFFERENCE

In his letter to the church at Ephesus, Paul said, "I pray that you, being rooted and established in love, may have power, together with all the saints, to grasp how wide and long and high and deep is the love of Christ, and to know this love that surpasses knowledge—*that you may be filled to the measure of all the fullness of God*" (Ephesians 3:17–19, author's emphasis). Do you suppose that being "filled up to the measure of the fullness of God" would cause you to display more godly character in your life? If so, how does that happen according to this verse? By striving in your own strength to be more godly? No, it is by understanding God's love—His great grace, if you will—for us. It is not a matter of beating on yourself and trying harder. Instead it is a matter of trusting God's mercy and grace. One key to developing godly character is recognizing it is God's work. Another key is beginning to grasp His love and grace toward us.

A sense of duty or guilt may cause a short-lived motivation in our lives, but it generally will not last. The only true, lasting motivation is God's love.

Peter said it this way: "But if anyone does not have [character qualities like perseverance, self-control, love, etc., mentioned in preceding verses] he is nearsighted and blind, and has forgotten that he has been cleansed from his past sins" (2 Peter 1:9). What is it that cleanses us from our sins? It is the grace of God, of course. This passage seems almost contradictory to our previous discussion. It sounds as though anyone who does not display these godly characteristics is being chastised. In reality this verse should be seen not as a condemning passage but as a diagnostic tool. The reason we don't have godly characteristics is because we have forgotten that we have been cleansed from our past sins. Hold on a minute. Why is forgetting that you have "been cleansed from your past sins" so devastating to growing in godly character?

I recall a period in my life when I was struggling with a particular recurring sin. I was devastated by the fact that I kept doing the same thing over and over. I was certain that God must no longer love me, or at the very least, He must be really, really unhappy with me. This attitude affected me even more than the sin itself. My relationship with God (through prayer, studying His Word, etc.) was suffering. This in turn affected my entire life. I displayed less and less godly character in my everyday activities. I had forgotten that I had been cleansed from my past sins.

If forgetting that our sins have been cleansed is the problem, then what is the solution? It would seem obvious that if the problem is forgetting, then the cure is remembering. That's what happened to me. I was reminded of the power of the cross. I remembered that I had "been cleansed from [my] past sins." I recalled the wondrous grace of God. When that happened, my relationship with God in all its fulness was restored, including the displaying of godly character. I was no longer beating on myself trying to be better. The real power source, God Himself, was again at work in me. That made all the difference.

Nearly 150 years ago Horatius Bonar, a Scottish pastor, phrased it like this:

> It is forgiveness that sets a man working for God. He does not work in order to be forgiven, but because he has been forgiven, and the consciousness of his sin being pardoned makes him long more for its entire removal than ever he did before.

An unforgiven man cannot work. He has not the will, nor the power, nor the liberty. He is in chains. Israel in Egypt could not serve Jehovah. "Let my people go that they may serve Me," was God's message to Pharaoh (Exodus 8:1): first liberty, then service.

A forgiven man is the true worker, the true lawkeeper. He can, he will, he must work for God. He has come into contact with that part of God's character which warms his cold heart. Forgiving love constrains him. He cannot but work for Him who has removed his sins from him as far as the east is from the west. Forgiveness has made him a free man, and given him a new and most loving Master. Forgiveness, received freely from the God and Father of our Lord Jesus Christ, acts as a spring, an impulse, a stimulus of divine potency. It is more irresistible than law, or terror, or threat.[1]

In his wonderful book *The Discipline of Grace*, Jerry Bridges made a simple little statement that had a powerful impact on my thinking: "Duty or guilt may motivate us for awhile, but only a sense of Christ's love for us will motivate us for a lifetime."[2] It's true. A sense of duty or guilt may cause a short-lived motivation in our lives, but it generally will not last. The only true, lasting motivation is God's love.

In Galatians 2:20 the apostle Paul said, "I have been crucified with Christ and I no longer live, but Christ lives in me. The life I live in the body, I live by faith in the Son of God, who loved me and gave himself for me." I recently heard someone suggest that this verse could be paraphrased like this: "If He loved me enough to give Himself for me, then He loves me enough to live out His life in me." Although this would probably be an oversimplification of this verse, the concept is accurate. We began our walk as believers founded totally on His grace and mercy. To endeavor to complete that walk on any other foundation would be error. Realizing the depth and strength of God's love and mercy toward us gives us the power to change and become more like Christ.

CHAPTER 20

GRATITUDE IS NOT ENOUGH

When someone does something for us that makes us feel special, our usual response is to reciprocate. We are motivated to offer kindness because of kindness received. Similarly there are those who would say that we should clean ourselves up—work harder and more diligently—out of gratitude toward God. After all, look what He has done for us. How could we not be grateful enough to put forth our best efforts for Him?

There are three major flaws in this ideology. First, our gratitude will ultimately only sustain us to a certain point. Our gratitude is not an unlimited commodity; we can only be grateful to a certain point. Our flesh stands in opposition to gratitude. The flesh's very presence, therefore, limits the depth and breadth of our gratefulness. When confronted by temptation, gratitude is generally only a minor deterrent. Our thankfulness to God certainly can be a curb to keep us on the right path, but it is only a small one. Given the right circumstances, we can easily ignore that obstacle of gratitude and wander off the right path into sin.

> *At times gratitude can be only a short curb that we will step right over, barely altering our stride.*

When you or I are tempted by that thing to which we are most vulnerable, gratitude is but a small help. Our gratefulness to God can, at times, seem like a giant, impenetrable wall. At other times, however, it can be only a short curb that we will step right over, barely altering our stride.

The truth is that no matter how grateful you are to God, that gratitude is too easily forgotten in the midst of temptation. When you are overcome by temptation and have fallen into sin, relying on your own merits to pull you out will not work. The only answer is to return to the grace of God. That is really the only answer that will ultimately make a difference in your life. No amount of self-will or gratitude will make the necessary changes in us. "*It is God* who arms me with strength and makes my way perfect. *He* makes my feet like the feet of a deer; *he* enables me to stand on the heights" (Psalm 18:32–33, author's emphasis).

I am not suggesting that gratitude has no value. We spent an entire chapter already talking about the fact that we should be grateful. However, it is reliance on *God's* mercy, not *our* gratefulness, that will cause us to become more like Him.

There is a second major flaw in basing our motivation to change on our gratefulness for what God has done in us. Without realizing it, our attempts to be better people can become a efforts to repay Jesus for what He did on the cross. Having been saved by grace, we try somehow to earn God's favor by changing how we live by our own strength. This will never work.

> *If we were somehow able to actually repay the Lord for what He has given us, then we have turned grace into a trade.*

In the first place, all that we have is from God. "Who has ever given to God, that God should repay him? For from Him and through Him and to Him are all things..." (Romans 11:35–36a). We cannot give anything to the Lord that He does not already have. Trying to repay God with what He already owns is futile.

Additionally, if we were somehow able to actually repay the Lord for what He has given us, then we have turned grace into a trade. "Now when a man works, his wages are not credited to him as a gift, but as an obligation" (Romans 4:4). When we barter with God, we have nullified His grace to us. Pastor John Piper said it like this: "If friends try to show you a special favor of love by having you over for dinner, and you end the evening by saying that you will pay them back by having them over next week, you nullify their grace and turn it into a trade."[1]

The third major flaw in this ideology is something we discussed earlier. If somehow our own gratitude causes us to become better people, then we can take credit for it. "No," you might argue, "it is gratitude to God." That's exactly my point. God is the object of the gratitude, not the source. The source for gratefulness is me. So even gratitude comes back to, "*I* will make myself a better person by being grateful." It won't work.

When we begin to understand God's great love and mercy toward us, we are grateful to Him. However, we cannot expect our gratefulness to motivate and cause us to change our lives to be more like Christ's. All the improvements in my life and yours clearly must be seen as the work of God in us, "for it is God who works in you to will and to act according to his good purpose" (Philippians 2:13).

CHAPTER 21

Do We Just Wait for God to Zap Us with Godly Character?

So what does all this mean? Can we just sit back with our feet up and wait for the Lord to zap us with godly character? Will there suddenly be a holy lightning bolt from the sky that will somehow change us into the perfected people God wants to make of us? Obviously this scenario is not the norm. Although God is powerful enough to do that, He generally does not.

One of my all-time favorite writers is C.S. Lewis. In his classic work *Mere Christianity*, Lewis said it this way:

> Handing everything over to Christ does not, of course, mean that you stop trying. To trust Him means, of course, trying to do all that He says. There would be no sense in saying you trusted a person if you would not take his advice. Thus if you have really handed yourself over to Him, it must follow that you are trying to obey Him. But trying in a new way, a less worried way. Not doing these things in order to be saved, but because He has begun to save you already. Not hoping to get to heaven as a reward for your actions, but inevitably wanting to act in a certain way because a first faint gleam of heaven is already inside you.[1]

Paul, writing to Titus, his "son in the faith" clearly tells us that, "It ["God's grace" mentioned in previous verse] teaches us to say 'No' to ungodliness and worldly passions, and to live self-controlled, upright and godly lives in this present age" (Titus 2:12). It is God's grace working in us that makes us different. However, Paul obviously recognized that this truth did not negate involvement on our part. Several verses later in the same letter Paul makes this statement: "I want you to stress these things, so that those who have trusted in God may be careful to *devote themselves to doing what is good*. These things are excellent and profitable for everyone" (Titus 3:8, author's emphasis). Yes, we should put forth our best efforts, but our best efforts must ultimately be understood as God's work in us.

It is essential to understand that there is an involvement on our part. Scripture tells us, "train yourself to be godly" (1 Timothy 4:7b). Seven times in the New Testament alone we are told to "Make every effort" Even Jesus frequently told people how to act in an acceptable manner. These and other passages from the Bible give us the understanding that we do not just sit and do nothing, waiting for God to make us better people. Clearly, we have a part to play. Highly-respected author and teacher Jerry Bridges uses the phrase "dependent responsibility." The balance between God's work in us and our work is found in being dependently responsible. We work in His strength. We are responsible to work, but we are completely dependent on the Lord.

> *The balance between God's work in us and our work is found in being dependently responsible. We are responsible to work, but we are completely dependent on the Lord.*

In his first letter to the church at Corinth, the apostle Paul talks about being the least of the apostles. He says, "I worked harder than all of them—yet not I, but the grace of God that was with me" (1 Corinthians 15:10). Paul recognized that even his best efforts were, in reality, God's work in him. He put forth his best effort, but he realized that even that was the work of the Lord.

In the classic book *The Christian's Secret of a Happy Life*, Hannah Whithall Smith shared an interesting perspective on this concept. She talked about a saw in a carpenter's shop:

> At one moment [we say] that the saw has sawn asunder a log, and the next moment declare that the carpenter has done it. The saw is the instrument used; the power that uses it is the carpenter's. And so we, yielding ourselves unto God, and our members as instruments of righteousness unto Him, find that He works in us to will and to do of His good pleasure, and we can say with Paul, "I laboured...yet not I, but the grace of God which was with me."[2]

> *My wife loves to garden. She has certain responsibilities in order for the gardens to be a success. However, there is clearly one thing she cannot do. She cannot make the plants grow.*

We, too, should put forth our best efforts. However, all of our efforts ultimately must be seen as not actually our own endeavors, but the work of God in us. Another quote from Jerry Bridges may be helpful here: "Although the Holy Spirit is the agent of sanctification and Himself works in us in this mysterious fashion, it is also true that He uses rational and understandable means to sanctify us."[3]

My wife loves to garden. We have several areas of our yard that are designated as vegetable or flower gardens. My wife has certain responsibilities in order for the gardens to be a success. Planting, watering, fertilizing, and weeding all are part of seeing a harvest from any garden. However, there is clearly one thing she cannot do. She cannot make the plants grow. She can provide a proper atmosphere for that to happen, but ultimately the growth is God's responsibility. The same is true in our lives. We clearly need to provide a proper atmosphere for growth, but the growth itself is the Lord's responsibility.

Over the next several chapters we will look at some the things through which the Lord can form a foundation on which godly character can be built. There are certain disciplines that we need to cultivate into our lives. In his classic book *Celebration of Discipline*, Richard Foster wrote, "God has given us the Disciplines of the spiritual life as a means of receiving His grace. The Disciplines allow us to place ourselves before God so that He can transform us."[4] These disciplines are not merely borne out of our own teeth-gritting determination. In light of all we've just read, these also must be recognized as the work of the Lord in our lives.

CHAPTER 22

SCRIPTURE STUDY AND MEMORIZATION

In order to go someplace unfamiliar, it is helpful to have a map. This is also true in developing godly character in our lives. We need to know what character is and understand it more fully in order to truly see it develop in our lives. One way that God develops godly character in us is through the study of His Word.

Someone once said that Scripture was not just given to increase your knowledge but to guide your conduct. It's true. As we read and study God's Word, it must be with an eye toward becoming more like Jesus. Increasing our understanding of God and His ways is good, but the real goal is to become more Christ-like.

The psalmist told us, "Your Word is a lamp to my feet and a light for my path" (Psalm 119:105). We need His Word to direct our steps and show us the proper ways to walk. When Scripture tells us, "Do this," or "Don't do this," it is acting like a road map, telling which ways are safest and best, and just as importantly, which paths to avoid. To walk out this life in a Christ-like manner, we definitely are in need of God's road map.

> *To walk out this life in a Christ-like manner we definitely are in need of God's road map.*

The apostle Paul wrote about "the knowledge of the truth that leads to godliness" (Titus 1:1). Obviously Paul expected that knowing the truth was going to cause a measure of godliness to be exhibited in God's people. Several times in his writings, Paul said, "Do you not know...?" Often it is a rebuke to cause his readers to recognize that those to whom the letter is addressed are not living the way they should. The expected result is that the readers will realize what it is they do not know (or are reminded of something they already know) and be changed because they now know it.

For example, Paul asked the church at Corinth, "Do you not know that your bodies are members of Christ

Himself? Shall I then take the members of Christ and unite them with a prostitute? Never!" (1 Corinthians 6:15). His obvious intent was to get them to look at this issue from a different angle. He apparently expected that gaining an alternate perspective would change not only the way they thought about the issue but also how they acted. Having the truth of God's Word ingrained in us will cause our thinking, and therefore our actions, to change. The more we study, learn, and memorize the Bible, the more God can work to form His character in us.

The psalmist said, "I have hidden your word in my heart that I might not sin against you." (Psalm 119:11). Later in the same psalm he reiterated the thought: "Direct my footsteps according to your word; let no sin rule over me" (Psalm 119:133).

I live near St. Louis, Missouri. Downtown, near the Mississippi River, there is a huge retaining wall. When the river overflows its banks, the retaining wall keeps the water in check, making sure it causes no destruction in the surrounding area. In much the same way, if we have the truth of God's Word within us, it acts just like that retaining wall, keeping sin in check and causing us to act the way we should.

Popular teacher and author Jack Hayford had this to say:

> For every question we face, we are not promised to find an immediate answer in the Bible. But as we feed on the Word daily, the wisdom we need for living our life is distilled in our soul. When we need it, though we may not remember chapters and verses, the strength and wisdom will be available in the spiritual resources inside us.[1]

The more of the Word of God we put on the inside, the more it will change us to be like Him. In his letter to the church in Rome, Paul tells us: "Do not conform any longer to the pattern of this world, *but be transformed by the renewing of your mind*" (Romans 12:2, author's emphasis). God's Word will cause that godly character to be formed in us, at least in part by changing our thinking. As we read and study the Bible and our thoughts begin to line up with His thoughts, then our lives will begin to be transformed by His power.

The Teacher's Commentary says it like this:

> As we apply what God has willed to our everyday lives, wisely letting God's Word guide our choices, we will live lives that are truly worthy of the Lord. In this process God Himself will be actively at work within and through us, producing the Holy Spirit's fruit in our personalities even as we are active in every good work.[2]

Some time ago I heard a speaker at a conference talking about the Word of God. During his message he referred to Psalm 107:20: "He sent forth his word and healed them." The speaker then posed the question, "Is this talking about the written Word or Jesus, the Word made flesh?" Among the few hundred people in attendance, there were those who were absolutely certain that one or the other was correct. The speaker said the correct answer to the question is "Yes." He went on to explain that we must understand that the two are inseparable. The Word of God is the Word of God, regardless of the form.

In John 14:6 Jesus told His followers that He is the truth. Later, in John 17:17, He is praying for His disciples. He asks the Father to "sanctify them by the truth; your *word* is truth" (author's emphasis). Since Jesus will soon no longer be visibly with them, it seems obvious that His prayer here is referring to the spoken/written Word of God. Both Jesus, the Word made flesh, and the spoken/written Word are truth and have power in our lives, "for you have exalted above all things your name and your word" (Psalm 138:2b).

The written Word of God is just as life-transforming as an in-the-flesh, personal encounter with Jesus. Unfortunately, because it is just ink on paper, we often place it on a much lower plane in our society. Oh, for the Church to have a revelation of the power and significance of the written Word of God!

Once we understand the value of the Word, we must regularly ingest it. Too many Christians depend solely on the weekly sermon at church for their intake of

The truth of God's Word acts just like that retaining wall, keeping sin in check and causing us to act the way we should.

God's Word. Mark Buchanan, in his book *Your God Is Too Safe*, said this:

> More and more people in our churches are food gluttons and biblical anorexics. Even our intake of Scripture has been reduced to a kind of fast-food drive-through, nibbling the crumbs tossed from the pulpit on Sunday. "I left that church. They just weren't feeding me."

When my son was eight, we taught him a discipline in keeping with his age. He would come home from school or some activity, flop on the couch, and yell, "I'm starving!" The discipline was to show him that there are certain foods he can help himself to—foods that are good for him, not just tasty—and *that he was fully capable of getting them himself.*

"I'm starving—this church isn't feeding me." Maybe that's a legitimate complaint from a three-year-old. From a grown-up, it's self-indictment.[3]

As Christians we must take the initiative to study and know God's Word for ourselves. Bible intake has been likened to eating food. However, it appears to me that there is one major difference: if we haven't eaten for awhile, we desire and crave food, but the less we read and study the Bible, the less we desire it. We must make it a priority in our lives.

Honest study and memorization of Scripture will give God the necessary platform to begin building godly character in our lives.

CHAPTER 23

PRAYER

A dear friend of mine is a teacher in the upper grades of high school. During her tenure she has encountered more than one "problem student." I'm sure you know what I mean. Every school—practically every classroom!—has at least one. These students are simply waiting for the opportunity to disrupt or sidetrack the class. I'm not talking about the person who occasionally simply interjects levity into the class setting. The true problem student is the one who wants to take over. Anything they can do to wrestle power from the instructor is acceptable. If they can railroad the discussion 180 degrees from the teacher's intended direction, then they are completely fulfilled.

My friend has told me that she always seems to spend far more time praying for the problem students than the others. Interestingly, though, through her prayers God builds a real compassion in her heart for those students. Through her prayers for others, God changes her.

Similarly God can use our intercession to build His character in our lives. As we pray for those around us, our hearts will become more and more open to the Lord's desires. In doing this, He is forming His character in us. Richard Foster said it this way:

> "You ask and do not receive, because you ask wrongly, to spend it on your passions" (James 4:3). To ask 'rightly' involves transformed passions, total renewal. In prayer, real prayer, we begin to think God's thoughts after Him: to desire the things He desires, to love the things He loves. Progressively we are taught to see things from His point of view.[1]

The Lord will begin building His character in us as we intercede for others, but we dare not stop there. We also need to pray for ourselves, that God would indeed build within us the godly characteristics He wants there. The Lord will work in us both through the *act of* prayer and the *answer to* prayer. He builds compassion for others, as well as other godly qualities in us, *as we pray,* and He also builds those qualities in us *as an answer* to our prayers.

During His earthly ministry Jesus demonstrated the priority of prayer. Luke 5:16 tells us, "But Jesus often withdrew to lonely places and prayed." The fact that the holy Son of God found it necessary to pray "often" should tell us something. And I find it interesting to note that neither the time nor the location of prayer seems to be extremely important. Jesus prayed in the morning (Mark 1:35), but He also prayed at night (Luke 6:12). He prayed outdoors and indoors. Jesus frequently prayed alone (Mark 1:35; 6:46; Luke 5:16; 6:12), but He sometimes prayed in groups (John 17) or even in crowds (Matthew 14:19; John 11:41–42).

Perhaps you are familiar with international evangelist Reinhard Bonnke. Hundreds of thousands of souls have come into the kingdom of God through his ministry. Bonnke credits a great measure of the success he has had to the people who consistently pray for him. Several years ago I heard the woman who leads the intercession team for Bonnke. Please understand that this is her job; she spends hours a day praying. However, she made one simple statement that has stuck with me ever since. She said, "It is not how long you pray or how 'powerfully' you pray—it is *that* you pray that counts."

> *I find it interesting to note that neither the time nor the location of prayer seems to be extremely important.*

Immediately after Jesus ascended into heaven, Scripture tell us, "They all joined together constantly in prayer" (Acts 1:14). This was what they thought was most important now that they were on their own. Jesus had apparently taught and demonstrated the value of prayer very well. They recognized that this was the thing that should now occupy their time. In fact, throughout the book of Acts, the theme of prayer in the life of the church is touched on more than thirty times. From an honest, biblical perspective there can be no doubt about the importance of God's people praying.

Jim Cymbala, pastor of the renowned Brooklyn Tabernacle, made this observation in his book *Fresh Wind, Fresh Fire*:

> Satan's main strategy with God's people has always been to whisper, 'Don't call, don't ask, don't depend on God to do great things. You'll get along fine if you just rely on your own cleverness and energy.' The truth of the matter is that the devil is not terribly frightened of our human efforts and credentials. But he knows his kingdom will be damaged when we lift up our hearts to God.[2]

Bob Sorge said, "There isn't a right way or a wrong way to cry out to God. Just cry! You need no tips or guidelines, just cry from the depths of your heart to Him. He hears His children."[3] In saying this, Sorge echoes the words of David from Psalm 34:15: "The eyes of the LORD are on the righteous and his ears are attentive to their cry."

Ultimately prayer is not so much about taking our wish list to God as it is a matter of relationship. Talk to the

Lord regularly and often. He has promised to hear and to answer. Here is just a very small smattering of promises about prayer from God's Word:

Ask and it will be given to you; seek and you will find; knock and it the door will be opened to you. For everyone who asks receives; he who seeks finds; and to him who knocks, the door will be opened (Matthew 7:7–8).

"If we felt certain of visible results within sixty seconds of every prayer, there would be holes in the knees of every pair of Christian-owned pants in the world!"

Before they call I will answer; while they are still speaking I will hear (Isaiah 65:24).

And if we know that he hears us—whatever we ask—we know that we have what we asked of Him (1 John 5:15).

You have granted him the desire of his heart and have not withheld the request of his lips (Psalm 21:2).

For everyone who asks receives; he who seeks finds; and to him who knocks, the door will be opened (Luke 11:10).

Given these promises (and scores of others) about the value of prayer, how could we not pray? In his book *Spiritual Disciplines of the Christian Life*, Donald Whitney made a powerful assertion:

> Often we do not pray because we doubt that any-
> thing will actually happen if we pray. Of course,
> we don't admit this publicly. But if we felt certain
> of visible results within sixty seconds of every
> prayer, there would be holes in the knees of every
> pair of Christian-owned pants in the world![4]

He's right. If we honestly took God at His Word, we would not need someone to prod us to spend time in prayer. If you haven't already done so, ask God right now to begin to cause you to recognize and act upon the power-ful discipline of prayer. As you pray, you will be changed to be more like Christ. He will instill His heart in you. You will grow in godly character.

CHAPTER 24

WORSHIP

O ver the years I have regularly been approached by people who have told me that honest, heart-felt worship of God has changed their lives in a dramatic way. Taking the time to honor the Lord through the discipline of worship causes our heart and spiritual eyes to be focused less on ourselves and more on God.

Acts 2:25 tells us that "David said about Him: 'I saw the Lord always before me. Because he is at my right hand, I will not be shaken.'" What an interesting statement. "I *saw* the Lord..." Did David literally *see* the Lord? Of course not. However, David was perhaps the prime Biblical example of a true worshiper. He chose to fill the frame of his life with the Lord, and because of this, there was no room left for doubt or despair. As we worship God, we become more and more focused on Who He is and think less and less about our own situations and circumstances.

From all we can ascertain in studying scriptural history, the prophet Isaiah was apparently one of the most godly, holy men of his time. But one day Isaiah encountered the holiest Being in the universe, and he suddenly became aware of his own unholiness.

> In the year that King Uzziah died, I saw the Lord seated on a throne, high and exalted, and the train of His robe filled the temple. Above Him were seraphs, each with six wings: With two wings they covered their faces, with two they covered their feet, and with two they were flying. And they were calling to one another: "Holy, holy, holy is the Lord Almighty; the whole earth is full of His glory." At the sound of their voices the doorposts and thresholds shook and the temple was filled with smoke. "Woe to me!" I cried. "I am ruined! For I am a man of unclean lips, and I live among a people of unclean lips, and my eyes have seen the King, the Lord Almighty" (Isaiah 6:1–5).

Please understand that Isaiah was a good guy. He was not part of the Mob. He did not rob banks. He was not involved in the pornography business. He did not worship false gods. He loved the Lord. But encountering the holiness of God made him suddenly aware of his own sinfulness. Look again at his response: "Woe to me! I am ruined!"

Throughout Scripture we see that prophets consistently used one of two words to begin their prophetic utterances: "blessed" or "woe." If they were speaking affirming words from God, they started by blessing the hearers. However, if the words were harsh, if they were rebuking the hearers, they started with "woe." Please realize that this is not just a cute little word with which to start off a negative statement. It actually

> *Isaiah was a good guy. He did not rob banks. He was not involved in the pornography business. But encountering the holiness of God made him suddenly aware of his own sinfulness. "Woe to me! I am ruined!"*

has the connotation of a curse (as opposed to a blessing). This was serious. Isaiah used this word on himself: "Woe to me!"

He went on to say, "I am ruined!" Other versions say things like, "My doom is sealed," "I am undone," or "I am lost." This was not a game for Isaiah. When he beheld the Lord, he realized anew his own sinfulness, so much so that he was certain that God would destroy him. The same thing happens in our own lives. When we encounter the reality of God, we recognize how far we are from His holiness. It stirs within us a desire to be changed.

The apostle John wrote, "But we know that when he appears, we shall be like him, for we shall see him as he is" (1 John 3:2). The more that I get to know God, the more I am convinced that this is not just a promise for the future but is true in part even now. In context this passage is obviously referring to the second coming of Jesus. However, it clearly tells us that the reason we shall be like Him is that "we shall see Him as He is." As we "behold the Lord" in worship, we are changed to be like Him.

One of my favorite songwriters is Mark Altrogge, a pastor in Indiana, Pennsylvania. Many of his songs have tremendously and positively influenced my walk with the Lord. In his song "The Love of a Holy God," Mark alludes to beholding God: "I'm ravished by one glance from Your loving eyes." While some have questioned the use of the word "ravished," I personally think it is perfect. It reminds me of Isaiah's experience of seeing the Lord in Isaiah 6. Remember his words? "I am ruined!" There is something about beholding the beauty of God that rips us apart and puts us back together even better than we were, all at the same time.

I am not suggesting that through a single encounter with the Lord your entire life will be forever perfect. It is possible but not normal. My experience has been that the more I gaze on the beauty of the Lord, the more I am conformed to His image. "We shall be like him for we shall see him." The more we spend time focusing on God in worship, the more we will become like Him.

The writer of the book of Hebrews tells us to "fix our eyes on Jesus..." (Hebrews 12:2). Can we actually *see* Jesus with our eyes? Again the answer is no. However, we can focus on the wonder of our God. We can make David's prayer in Psalm 27 our own prayer. "One thing I ask of the LORD, this is what I seek: that I may dwell in the house of the LORD all the days of my life, *to gaze upon the beauty of the LORD and to seek him in his temple*" (Psalm 27:4, author's emphasis).

As we spend time worshiping God—individually or corporately—we are choosing to look to Him. As we do so, the Lord will cause us to become more and more like Him. The discipline of worship will cause more of His character to be developed in us.

CHAPTER 25

MAKING RIGHT CHOICES

Many believe Elijah to be the greatest prophet of the Old Testament. God used Elijah to raise a widow's son back to life (1 Kings 17:22). Elijah was the one who confronted the prophets of Baal on Mount Carmel and, in doing so, caused the people of Israel to turn back to the Lord (1 Kings 18:16–40). Elijah was greatly used by God in many ways. However, it was Elijah's servant,

Elisha, who received a "double portion" of Elijah's anointing (2 Kings 2:9). It was Elisha who, among other things, caused an axhead to float (2 Kings 6:6), raised a child from the dead (2 Kings 4:8–37), and even captured an entire army (2 Kings 6:8–23). Because of this, it would seem that Elisha's servant, Gehazi (pronounced *gay-khah-zee´*), was poised to become the next great prophet of Israel. The story in 2 Kings mentions Gehazi no less than twenty times. He had everything going for him. Just as Elisha had learned from his day-to-day interaction with Elijah, so Gehazi was learning from Elisha. He had a tremendous future.

Gehazi had the best preparation possible for ministry training. He was being made ready to take over the office of prophet in Israel. Yet he was lacking in character, and that disqualified him.

In the Bible God frequently had one person train or mentor another, and along with the external training (how to preach a good sermon, etc.) would come spiritual blessings from God. A good example is how Jesus taught His disciples. He gave them practical training and then gave them the spiritual authority they needed to multiply the ministry.

The classic example of this in the Old Testament is Elijah and Elisha. Elijah taught Elisha, and then God gave him the spiritual power he needed to carry on the ministry in an even greater way. The people in that culture recognized this progression. They understood that this was how God dealt with the people; spiritual authority, as such, was passed along just like royal authority. It could be expected to pass from Elijah to Elisha, and then from Elisha to Gehazi.

That's why in 2 Kings 3:11, when the kings of Judah, Israel, and Edom were looking for a prophet—someone to give them a word from God—one of the army officers said, "Elisha son of Shaphat is here. He used to pour water on the hands of Elijah." Pour water on the hands?! So what?! So everything. It was understood in that culture that spiritual authority was handed down, passed along. The army officer didn't think this statement was odd. Neither did those who heard it. They immediately summoned Elisha.

Sometime later, along came Naaman, the commander of the army of the king of Aram. Naaman had leprosy. His servant suggested to him that this great Israelite prophet, Elisha, would possibly be able to heal him. So Naaman went to Israel to find Elisha and seek healing. After an interesting interaction (check it out for yourself in 2 Kings 5), Naaman was healed. In gratefulness for his health being restored, Naaman offered Elisha a handsome reward—10 talents (about 750 pounds) of silver, 6,000 shekels (about 150 pounds) of gold, and ten sets of clothing. Elisha, however, refused it all. "As surely as the LORD lives, whom I serve, I will not accept a thing" (2 Kings 5:16). Naaman pressured further, but Elisha still refused. Finally Naaman left.

Then we learn the truth about the character of Gehazi, Elisha's servant.

> After Naaman had traveled some distance, Gehazi, the servant of Elisha the man of God, said to himself, "My master was too easy on Naaman, this Aramean, by not accepting from him what he brought. As surely as the LORD lives, I will run after him and get something from him."
>
> So Gehazi hurried after Naaman. When Naaman saw him running toward him, he got down from the chariot to meet him. "Is everything all right?" he asked.
>
> "Everything is all right," Gehazi answered. "My master sent me to say, 'Two young men from the company of the prophets have just come to me from the hill country of Ephraim. Please give them a talent of silver and two sets of clothing.'"
>
> "By all means, take two talents," said Naaman. He urged Gehazi to accept them, and then tied up the two talents of silver in two bags, with two sets of clothing. He gave them to two of his servants, and they carried them ahead of Gehazi.
>
> When Gehazi came to the hill, he took the things from the servants and put them away in the house. He sent the men away and they left. Then he went in and stood before his master Elisha.
>
> "Where have you been, Gehazi?" Elisha asked.
>
> "Your servant didn't go anywhere," Gehazi answered.
>
> But Elisha said to him, "Was not my spirit with you when the man got down from his chariot

to meet you? Is this the time to take money, or to accept clothes, olive groves, vineyards, flocks, herds, or menservants and maidservants? Naaman's leprosy will cling to you and to your descendants forever."

Then Gehazi went from Elisha's presence and he was leprous, as white as snow (2 Kings 5:19–27).

Gehazi had everything going for him. He was poised to become the next great prophet of Israel. After what Elijah had accomplished and the miracles Elisha had done, what could the name of Gehazi have been in the historical record of Israel? He was destined for greatness. But he gave it all up because of greed. He traded it all away for the door marked "Worldly Pleasures."

Gehazi had the best preparation possible for ministry training. He was being made ready to take over the office of prophet in Israel. Yet he was lacking in character, and that disqualified him. We see that is takes godly character to make godly decisions.

Our wrong decisions can sometimes have serious consequences. Although there is forgiveness, forgiveness does not always remove the consequences of our words and actions. For example, what would have happened if:

Eve had not listened to the serpent? (Genesis 3:1–6)

All twelve of the Israelite spies had come back with an encouraging report of the promised land? (Numbers 13:27–33)

David had looked away and left the roof-top rather than look at Bathsheba bathing? (2 Samuel 11:2)

The rich young ruler had obeyed Jesus and willingly given away his wealth to the poor? (Matthew 19:16–22)

We may not realize when we face a defining moment in our life because it may seem to come out of nowhere. Such tests of our character are often well past before we recognize their significance. Therefore, our everyday choices not only determine but also reveal our character.

In what I believe is an amazingly succinct synopsis of this issue, former Indiana U.S. Senator Dan Coats said this:

Character cannot be summoned at the moment of crisis if it has been squandered by years of compromise and rationalization. The only testing ground for the heroic is the mundane. The only preparation for that one profound decision which can change a life, or even a nation, is those hundreds of half-conscious, self-defining, seemingly insignificant decisions made in private.

In his book *Reaching for the Invisible God*, Philip Yancey discusses the concept of training ourselves to be godly.

Church history yields many examples of people who took spiritual disciplines to an unhealthy extreme, mortifying their bodies and shunning all pleasures. We rightly recoil from such extremes. Yet as I read their accounts now I note that these "spiritual athletes" were acting voluntarily, and few looked back on their experiences with much regret. We live in a society that cannot comprehend those who fast or carve out two hours for a quiet time, and yet honors professional football players who work out with weights five hours a day and undergo a dozen knee and shoulder surgeries to repair the damage they inflict upon themselves in the sport. Our aversion to spiritual discipline may reveal more about ourselves than about the "saints" we criticize.[1]

> *"Watch your choices, they become your actions. Watch your actions, they become your habits. Watch your habits, they become your character."*

My youngest son Stephen is taking drum lessons. I regularly tell him that if he really wants to be a good drummer he must spend time practicing. If he makes the decision to run off and frolic when he should be working on learning how to play better, he will pay the price later in not being as skilled on the drums. Just as the choices Stephen makes now will significantly affect his development as a drummer, the choices we make now will significantly affect the development of our character

I recently came across a statement that is rather profound: "Watch your choices, they become your actions.

Watch your actions, they become your habits. Watch your habits, they become your character." It's true. What on the surface appears to be only one, small, insignificant choice could in reality be far more. We must recognize how absolutely essential making right, godly choices is to developing godly character.

CHAPTER 26

YIELDING TO GOD

I fly a lot. I consider myself very fortunate in that I have never completely lost any baggage. Although I have encountered people who have lost luggage, mine has always eventually turned up.

There are at least two ways to lose luggage when traveling by air. The first is to leave your bag unattended in the airport and have someone walk off with it. If that were to happen, the scene might look something like this:

Returning from the restroom, I find my bag gone. I approach the gate agent and explain that my bag is missing. He might request a description of the bag and its general contents. He will most certainly ask where I saw it last.

"I left it right over there on that seat when I went to use the restroom, and now it's gone."

"Oh, I see," he responds. "Well, I could make an announcement about it and see if anyone turns it in. However, it is much more likely that your bag really is gone." He is not going to expend much energy to help when he realizes that my carelessness is the reason my bag is missing.

> *The problem with a living sacrifice is that it keeps crawling off the altar.*

The other way to lose luggage is when the airline misplaces it. I've had this happen. When I explain where I've come from and show my baggage claim receipts, the airline employees willingly bend over backward to help. They request an address where I will be staying and promise to have the bag(s) delivered either later that day or the next morning—at the airline's expense. This scenario is very different from the first one. Why? Because I have entrusted my luggage into their care and they are now responsible for it.

When we entrust ourselves to God, we become His responsibility—"because I know whom I have believed, and am convinced that he is able to guard what I have *entrusted* to him for that day" (2 Timothy 1:12b, author's emphasis). We must yield ourselves into His hands, trusting His faithfulness to keep us.

However, it is clear from Scripture that this is not simply a once-and-for-all action. It must be repeated consistently. Entrusting ourselves to the Lord in general is good. We recognize that "You are not your own; you were bought at a price" (1 Corinthians 6:19b–20a). This overall yielding to Him is important, but there must also come a consistent yielding to Him to fully walk in submission.

Paul the apostle said, "Therefore, I urge you, brothers, in view of God's mercy, to *offer your bodies as living sacrifices*, holy and pleasing to God" (Romans 12:1, author's emphasis). I like to think of doing this on a daily basis. What would happen if each day when you awaken you were to pray something along these lines: "Lord, today I'm Yours. Wherever I go, whatever I do, I want You to be glorified in my life. I willingly yield myself to You and ask that You would work in and through me"? Would honestly praying something like that in a true, heartfelt way each morning make a difference in your life? Of course it would.

Clearly we are to offer our "bodies as living sacrifices," but this in and of itself is not enough. Someone once commented that the problem with a living sacrifice is that it keeps crawling off the altar. Have you found this to be true in your own life? Besides a general yielding and even a daily yielding there needs to be a consistent, ongoing giving ourselves to God.

In the Garden of Gethsemane, three times Jesus committed Himself to His Father, praying "not as I will, but as you will" (Matthew 26:39), and "may your will be done" (Matthew 26:42). Jesus was clearly committed to His

Father, but He further entrusted this specific time in His life to God.

Throughout that day and into the next, Jesus' situation grew even more intense. The questionings, the insults, the humiliation, the beatings, and finally the cross—this must have been highly emotional and difficult time for Jesus. Peter sums up Jesus' reaction in his first letter: "When they hurled their insults at him, he did not retaliate; when he suffered, he made no threats. Instead, *he entrusted himself to him who judges justly*" (1 Peter 2:23, author's emphasis).

We need to do that. Regularly, on an ongoing basis, we should entrust ourselves to the Lord. He has promised to lead us as we commit our ways to Him. "Commit to the LORD whatever you do, and your plans will succeed" (Proverbs 16:3). "In all your ways acknowledge him [the LORD], and he will make your paths straight" (Proverbs 3:6).

When we entrust ourselves to the Lord, He is free to work in us. Like the airline employee who diligently searches for the luggage that was entrusted to his care, so 2 Timothy 1:12 promises us that God will take care of the things we entrust to Him.

Consistently yielding to God throughout the course of our days gives Him more opportunity to work in and through us. Instead of being the living sacrifices with that tendency to crawl off the altar, we become committed to Him. His plans become our plans. His thoughts become our thoughts. His will—like Jesus prayed in Gethsemane—becomes our will. Regularly entrusting ourselves into God's hands will give Him greater access to us. In other words, He will have more opportunity to build His character in us.

CHAPTER 27

ACCOUNTABILITY

I am part of a small accountability group. Two other men and I meet together each week. We pray together, study the Word, and are totally honest with one another about our walk with the Lord and its triumphs and failures. We know each other well. We know one another's areas of struggle. We rejoice with each other in triumphs. We hold one another accountable to scriptural standards for life.*

Accountability is a hot topic in the church today. After seeing several high-profile leaders stumble and fall, we would do well to recognize our need for accountability. However, please realize that even though this issue is getting a lot of press recently, it is certainly not a new concept in the church. The Bible tells us, "Therefore confess your sins to each other and pray for each other so that you may be healed" (James 5:16a).

> *We pray together, study the Word, and are totally honest with one another about our walk with the Lord and its triumphs and our failures.*

There is clearly something about confessing our sins "to each other" that takes it beyond simply confessing our sins to God. Uh, oh. I can already envision the letters from Protestants asking, "Are you suggesting that we begin some sort of confessional process like the Roman Catholics?" No. However, I would like to suggest that having someone with whom you can be completely candid—someone who is able to press an

---

*In case you're interested in starting such a group, I thought I should share a couple of details. I actually began this group after reaching a point in my life where I realized how beneficial being honestly accountable to others would be. I chose a couple of dear friends who I knew cared deeply for me and were also bold enough to be honest with me and actually hold me accountable.

issue with you and not feel out of line—can be very good for you. It takes repentance to a deeper level. I can confess my sin to God and be forgiven. However, when I repent openly to others, there is a deeper accountability and sense of freedom. Nothing is hidden.

Part of the reason that accountability can be effective is that we realize that we need to be totally honest with the other person(s). We as humans are generally not as forgiving as God. When I admit my sin to the Lord, I know He will still love me and offer forgiveness. With my accountability partners there is always a dimension of uncertainty, even though they have never given me any reason to be uncertain. In part it may be that I am keenly aware of my own nature to be less than forgiving at times.

This type of relationship should be a vital ingredient in all our lives. Spending time with others, talking, sharing, and listening should be a normal part of life for us as believers. A while back I heard a pastor read a poem. Unfortunately he did not know the source of the poem (someone had read it to him), but I quickly wrote it down as he read it:

> Oh the comfort of feeling safe with a person,
> Having neither to weigh thought nor measure
>   word
> But letting it all out, chaff and grain together;
> Knowing that a faithful friend will sift it
> And keep what is worth keeping,   ·
> And, with a breath of mercy, blow the rest away.
>   © unknown

We all need friends like that. No masks. No pretending. People we can be real with. This poem reminds me of some of the words of Solomon: "Wounds from a friend can be trusted" (Proverbs 27:6) True friends are not out to get us. Often close friends speak truth that wounds our fragile pride, but since we rest assured that they have our best in mind, we can accept what they have said. "The pleasantness of one's friend springs from his earnest counsel" (Proverbs 27:9). A real friend will not hold back the truth. He is earnest, and that is good.

The apostle Paul had many friends. His friends took care of him while he was in prison (Acts 24:23; 27:3). He regularly referred to various close friends in his letters, extending greetings from them or asking that greetings be extended to them. He even refers to some as his "dear friends," like Timothy, Luke, and Gaius. If Paul, great man of faith that he was, found it necessary to have close friends, should not we also consider this a high priority?

Please understand that I am not talking about having close, intimate relationships with everyone you know. There are various levels of relationships. Even Jesus demonstrated this. There were multitudes that followed Him, but He had twelve that were closest to Him. Of these, there were three, Peter, James, and John, that comprised Jesus' inner circle. Even beyond this, the Bible refers to John as "the disciple that Jesus loved" (John 13:23; 19:26; 20:2; 21:7; 21:20). Jesus did not have the same closeness with everyone that He did with John.

The same is true for us. We will not have the same depth in all of our relationships. The guys with whom I am accountable are just two among scores of people I would call friends. However, those two make a huge difference in my life.

Near the beginning of this chapter I mentioned the words of the apostle James: "Therefore confess your sins to each other and pray for each other so that you may be healed" (James 5:16a). It is vital to understand that just the confession alone is not enough. We must also pray for one another. That is where we will see the real victories won. However, the prerequisite to the prayer is to have an honest enough relationship to admit what it is for which you need prayer.

What about you? Are you honestly accountable to another person or persons? Can you share absolutely anything with them? If not, isn't it time you considered developing a relationship like that?

CHAPTER 28

GOD'S OTHER METHOD: ADVERSITY

B eyond the spiritual disciplines we have discussed (and please understand this was not an exhaustive list), what other methods does God use to instill His character in us? If you are honestly interested in the answer to that question, then keep reading. You may not like the answer, though. Let's look at what the Bible has to say.

"Not only so, but we also rejoice" (I like rejoicing) "in our sufferings," (hey, wait a minute—rejoice in our sufferings?) "because we know that suffering produces perseverance; perseverance, character..." (Romans 5:3–4). Ummm, I'm not too excited about that passage. Let's try another one.

"Consider it pure joy, my brothers" (okay, joy is a good thing) "whenever you face trials of many kinds" (joy in trials?!) "because you know that the testing of your faith develops perseverance. Perseverance must finish its work so that you may be mature and complete, not lacking anything" (James 1:2–4). I really don't like the way this is going so far, but let's look at one more section of Scripture.

"In this you greatly rejoice" (I still like rejoicing but I'm starting to get a little nervous when I see that word now), "though now for a little while you may have had to suffer grief in all kinds of trials" (I knew it! It's the "suffer" and "trials" thing again). "These things have come so that your faith—of greater worth than gold, which perishes even though refined by fire—may be proved genuine and may result in praise, glory and honor when Jesus Christ is revealed" (1 Peter 1:6–7).

Are you seeing a pattern here? Robert Moeller, in his wonderful book *Love in Action*, said it like this: "What happens in us is more important to God than what happens to us. The development of a Christ-like character is God's first and foremost agenda for our lives. For that to happen, we sometimes go through difficult situations"[1] In short, building character requires things like perseverance, endurance, patience, and even the "s" word, suffering.

Many believers today have the idea that as Christians we should not suffer. That sounds like a nice idea in theory, but it is blatantly opposed to the full counsel of the Word of God, as we have just read.

> *If it were true that following the Lord would negate any problems, then the apostle Paul spent most of his life outside of God's will.*

If anyone is to go into captivity, into captivity he will go. If anyone is to be killed with the sword, with the sword he will be killed. This calls for patient endurance and faithfulness on the part *of the saints* (Revelation 13:10, author's emphasis).

Unfortunately, because of the idea that Christians shouldn't suffer, we have too often equated difficulty in the life of a fellow-believer with some sort of sin in that person's life. We may say, "There must be some reason God is allowing them to go through that." That could be true, but then again, it might not be true. The reality is that sometimes we experience the results of sin, not because of our own sin but simply because we live in a sinful world.

Our family lives near the most dangerous stretch of highway in the state of Missouri. Not long ago a woman was killed on that highway in a head-on crash with a drunk driver. The woman was not even slightly at fault. It was 100% the responsibility of the other driver. What did the woman do to deserve that? Nothing. Yet because we live in a sinful world, we will sometimes reap the results of sin in general.

Even though this is true, however, there is a powerful verse of Scripture that we need to recall in such situations. Romans 8:28 says, "And we know that in almost all things..." Wait a minute! That passage does not say *almost* all things. Let's try again. "And we know that in *all* (author's emphasis) things God works for the good of those who love him, who have been called according to his purpose." We may not always understand it. We may not always see the ultimate plan. However, the One Who sees the end from the very beginning knows exactly what is going on every step of the way, and He will work *all* things for our good.

Some folks believe that as long as you are following God's plan and doing exactly what the Lord wants you to do, then everything in your life is going to be great. Wrong!

In Mark 4:35–38 the disciples obeyed Jesus and found themselves in the midst of a storm so severe they were certain they were going to die. This is not exactly the scenario one would expect if obedience to God equals the ideal life. Even Jesus suffered, but it was obviously not because of sin in His life. His suffering was part of the plan of God.

If it were true that following the Lord would negate any problems, then the apostle Paul spent most of his life outside of God's will. He was constantly having problems.

Paul had more difficult situations in his life than most entire congregations in our country have gone through collectively. He was whipped on five different occasions, beaten with rods three times, stoned and left for dead, shipwrecked three times, and even spent a day and a night in the open sea, not to mention the numerous times he was threatened—all because he *was* living God's plan for his life.

Everyone knows that Paul talked about his "thorn in the flesh." However, do you know why he had it? Paul explained it like this: "To keep me from becoming conceited because of these surpassingly great revelations, there was given me a thorn in the flesh, a messenger of Satan, to torment me" (2 Corinthians 12:7). God had revealed so many of His plans and purposes to Paul that Paul needed a thorn in the flesh to keep him from becoming conceited. It was not because he was doing anything wrong. In fact, it appears to be because Paul was doing so much right. The thorn in the flesh was not because of wrongdoing but because of right-doing.

I am certainly not suggesting that all suffering is from God. However, I would be in error to proclaim that suffering is never part of the Lord's plan. "So then, those who suffer *according to God's will* should commit themselves to their faithful Creator and continue to do good" (1 Peter 4:19, author's emphasis). "Suffer according to God's will." That's pretty clear.

If you were to choose one of Jesus' twelve original apostles who would be able to talk from experience about the always-victorious, overcoming life, whom would you pick? I'll give you a hint. According to history ten of the remaining eleven (after Judas betrayed Jesus) died a martyr's death. Only one survived to an old age: John. Of all those hand-picked disciples, John would be top choice for sharing on the subject "The Real Christian Life, The Way Things Oughta Be."

However, as John prepared to share the vision God had given him, he said, "I, John, your brother and companion in the *suffering* and kingdom and *patient endurance* that are ours in Jesus, was on the island of Patmos" (Revelation 1:9, author's emphasis). "Suffering"? "Patient endurance"? "That are *ours*"? "In Jesus"? Because of our faith in Him, we sometimes suffer. That's not what we want to hear about. Well, we may not want to hear it, but it's reality.

> *Godly character is formed during difficult times. Those less-than-positive situations deepen our foundation in God.*

In his second letter to the Thessalonian church, Paul makes an interesting statement: "Therefore, among God's churches we boast about your perseverance and faith in all the persecutions and trials you are enduring" (2 Thes-salonians 1:4).

I find it fascinating to note that Paul does not say he is boasting about how God has kept them in perfect health. He does not indicate any bragging about the way the Lord blessed them financially. No, instead Paul boasts about the "perseverance and faith in all the persecutions and trials" they are enduring. There is no indication that Paul considers the persecutions and trials to be odd. He apparently saw this as a normal part of life. However, the thing that excited Paul was the perseverance and faith that were being built because of the difficult times.

The important point to recognize in all of this is that regardless of the origin of the difficulty, if we let Him, God will use *all* suffering to form His character in us. Consider the J.B. Phillips rendering of James 1:2–4: "When all kinds of trials crowd into your lives, my brothers, don't resent them as intruders, but welcome them as friends! Realize that they have come to test your endurance. But let the process go on until that endurance is fully developed, and you will find you have become men [and women] of mature character."

Godly character is formed during difficult times. Those less-than-positive situations deepen our foundation in God. A house of cards is easily blown down. An earthquake-proof building has steel piers driven all the way down to solid rock. Driving those steel piers that far into the rock takes a lot of pressure, but it is worth the effort because it makes the foundation stronger. That's how the Lord uses difficult times in our lives. "Before I was afflicted I went astray, but now I obey Your Word... It was good for me to be afflicted so that I might learn Your decrees" (Psalm 119:67, 71).

Although God wants us to succeed, He will not cause that to happen at the expense of our spiritual health. Jesus told us, "I am the true vine, and my Father is the gardener...every branch that does bear fruit He prunes so that it will be even more fruitful" (John 15:1–2). Ask anyone who has studied the effects of pruning on a tree. There is usually some sort of trauma involved on the part of the tree. The tree "reacts" to the pruning. It apparently is not pleasant. However, the long-term effects will be very positive. Jesus promised that we would be pruned. He also promised that the pruning process would ultimately make us more fruitful.

Years ago I heard a man talking about the process used to refine gold. I'm not certain it is still done the same way today, but this was an older man who had been a smith (silver and gold) for years. He told of heating the gold until it became liquid. As the gold heated, the impurities (the dross) rose to the top. These impurities were skimmed off and soon more dross rose to the top. It was a rather lengthy process and required a great measure of patience. The final indication to the goldsmith that the gold was pure was that he could see his face reflected in the surface of the gold. That's what God does in our lives. He keeps turning up the heat and patiently skimming off the impurities. His goal is to see His character, Christ-likeness, formed in us.

Frances Jane Crosby was born in 1820. When she was barely a month old, her parents noticed a serious problem with her eyes. Unfortunately the community doctor was away. In desperation her family sought out a man who claimed to be a physician. The "doctor" insisted that extreme heat would draw out the infection so he put a hot poultice on her eyes. Years later other doctors diagnosed Crosby's blindness as having been caused by the incompetent treatment.

In spite of her blindness, Frances Jane—more commonly known as Fanny—Crosby went on to write more than 9,000 Christian hymns. Her poetry and her speaking influenced hundreds of thousands of people.

> Far from feeling self-pity, Fanny felt that on the whole, blindness was a special gift of God. She often said, "It was the best thing that could have happened to me," and, "How in the world could I have lived such a helpful life as I have lived had I not been blind?" She felt she would never have had the opportunity for an education had she not been blind. Had she not gone to the Institution

[for the blind] in New York, she would not have
had the contacts to enable her to write hymns for
a nationally known publishing firm.

Moreover she believed that sight must be a
distraction. She attributed her great powers of
concentration to blindness. She also felt that her
lack of sight enabled her to develop a wonderful
memory and enhanced her appeal as a speaker,
creating a bond of sympathy between her and her
audiences that made them more receptive to the
Gospel message.[2]

Fanny had a very interesting perspective on the
entire situation. "She knew there was always a good reason for affliction. She would often quote Hebrews 12:6,
saying, 'Whom the Lord loveth, He chasteneth,' and com-
menting, 'If I had no troubles, I'd think the Lord didn't
love me!'"[3]

Difficult times can either push us away from God or
closer to Him. The apostle Paul said, "We do not want you
to be uninformed, brothers, about the hardships we suffered in the province of Asia. We were under great pressure,
far beyond our ability to endure, so that we despaired even
of life. Indeed, in our hearts we felt the sentence of death.
But this happened that we might not rely on ourselves but on God,
who raises the dead" (2 Corinthians 1:8–9, author's emphasis). Hardships drove them to Jesus.

Scripture says this about Jesus in the Garden of
Gethsemane: "And being in anguish, he prayed more
earnestly" (Luke 22:44). Jesus allowed His anguish to push
Him *toward* the Father, not away. Every trial we walk through
is a place of decision for us. Those difficult times can repel us

away from the Lord. Or we can choose to draw closer to Him, and in doing so, allow Him to form His character in us.

My wife recently attended a women's retreat where the main speaker invited them to chart their spiritual lives. She asked them to recall high and low points during their lives and see if they could draw any conclusions. My wife noticed that it was at the very times when she was going through turmoil that she had the greatest spiritual growth.

> *Difficult times can either push us away from God or closer to Him.*

God used those difficult situations to cause her to come to a higher level of maturity in Him.

For several years my family and I have enjoyed a theme park called Silver Dollar City in Branson, Missouri. Besides the fun rides and family atmosphere, there are numerous old-time craft demonstrations, such as basket-weaving, candy-making, and glass-blowing. One of the exhibits I find fascinating is the blacksmith shop. You probably recall seeing a blacksmith working in an old Western movie. A piece of iron is heated to the point where it glows white-hot. Then the smith puts the metal on an anvil and pounds it with a hammer. Sparks fly as he attacks the glowing piece of iron. The smith uses intense heat and lots of pressure to shape that piece of iron into something useful. Similarly God frequently uses intense heat and lots of pressure to shape and transform us into the image of Jesus.

CHAPTER 29

PATIENCE—THE PROCESS

In Frank Peretti's book *The Visitation*, one of the characters, Travis Jordan, reflected on a recent incident:

> I tried to remind myself, "Hey, time is one of
> God's primary tools for teaching wisdom." Time.
> And more time. And still more time. More pray-
> ing, more asking, more weeks, months, or even

years of anguish trying to pull it all together. This
frustrating little session on the hill reminded me
of something I'd learned over the years: God
won't be hurried.[1]

The great Old Testament leader Moses was raised in
Pharaoh's household. Pharaoh was the king of what
appears to be the most culturally advanced society on earth
in that day. Having been brought up in the king's home,
Moses would have received the very best education possible. In that culture he would have been taught everything
from academics to art, the sciences to sports. Even things
like the art of war would have been considered proper education for a young man in the king's household. "Moses
was educated in all the wisdom of the Egyptians and was
powerful in speech and action" (Acts 7:22).

With that type of education, when Moses slew the
Egyptian (Exodus 2:12), he had the wherewithal to lead the
Israelites out of Egypt. He could have done it. But God
said, "Not yet. First you need to spend forty years in the
desert." Forty years in the desert?! From an educational
perspective, what did Moses learn during that time that he
hadn't already learned in his formal schooling process?
Probably not much. However, those forty years made him a
much different person than the hot-headed avenger he had
been in his younger days. God built the necessary character
traits into Moses through a process of waiting.

It is by faith and patience that we inherit the promises
of God. "We do not want you to become lazy, but to imitate
those who through faith and patience inherit what has been
promised" (Hebrews 6:12). Consider this: How long after
God (through Samuel) anointed David as king did David

actually become the king of Israel? It was ten to twelve years. How long after God called Paul did the great apostle actually leave on his first missionary journey? Again, it was ten or eleven years. What about Joseph of the Old Testament waiting for his dream (a dream from God, no less) to be fulfilled?

It was a period of many years and much heartache. How long did Abraham wait for God to fulfill the promise that Abraham would be father of many nations? Decades rolled past before the fulfillment even began to take place.

In each of these God could have fulfilled the promise immediately. Would that have been too difficult for the Lord? Obviously not. The Lord is powerful enough to cause any or all

When Moses slew the Egyptian (Exodus 2:12) he had the wherewithal to lead the Israelites out of Egypt. But God said, "Not yet."

of those things to happen in a moment. In the ensuing time of waiting, however, He was building something far more important than the actual fulfillment into the hearts and lives of the people. Their character was being developed.

This whole idea of patience is completely foreign in our society. We want everything *now*. You can drive through practically anything in our country, and if you don't have the necessary funds to pay for it, don't worry. Just pull out your credit card, and you can have it anyway. Patience seems to be totally unnecessary. However, the kingdom of God does not generally work that way.

> Be patient, then, brothers, until the Lord's com-
> ing. See how the farmer waits for the land to yield
> its valuable crop and how patient he is for the
> autumn and spring rains. You too, be patient and
> stand firm, because the Lord's coming is near...
> Brothers, as an example of patience in the face of
> suffering, take the prophets who spoke in the
> name of the Lord. As you know, we consider
> blessed those who have persevered. You have
> heard of Job's perseverance and have seen what
> the Lord finally brought about. The Lord is full of
> compassion and mercy (James 5:7–8, 10–11).

I frequently teach seminars on developing the music and worship ministry of churches. In these I often take time to share about the way God has blessed the music ministry in our little church. We have some extremely gifted musicians who love God with all their hearts. As I share about these things, it is not at all unusual for people to ask me to pray for them to have at their church what we have at ours. There is just one problem, however. They want tomorrow what we have spent two decades building. It certainly could happen, but probably will not.

Jesus taught a couple of parables that seem appropriate here. You are probably familiar with the Parable of the Talents (Matthew 25:14–30) and the Parable of the Minas (Luke 19:11–27). In each the lead character is an apparently wealthy man who is going to be gone for a long time. He turns his money over to his servants to manage while he is gone. In both stories there were some servants who took good care of their master's money through wise investments and earned a handsome increase. Because of their good stewardship of the master's money, they were richly rewarded. However, in each parable there was one servant who did nothing with what the master had given and was consequently rebuked upon the master's return.

I wish Jesus had given a few more specifics in these parables. Neither story tells how long the master was gone, or more specifically, how long the servants were expected to be good stewards of that which had been entrusted to them. In neither story are we told exactly what the final reward is. I wish Jesus had indicated that if we were faithful with ____ (a specific thing) for ____ (a specific amount of time) then we would get ____ (a specific reward). Adding in specifics like that would make those parables much more to my liking. But Jesus didn't do that.

The most common entry in Christopher Columbus' journal was, "Today we sailed on." Some days—most days —are like that in life.

In these parables there is an obvious indication that if we are faithful over a long period of time we will receive a reward of some type. ("Well done, good and faithful servant! You have been faithful with a few things; I will put you in charge of many things.") The clear understanding is that we simply are to keep being faithful, not just doing it for a certain length of time and then stopping. We must keep on going. "And as for you, brothers, never tire of doing what is right" (2 Thessalonians 3:13). You may be more familiar with King James Version of this verse, "Be not weary in well doing." In today's vernacular we would say, "Just keep doing the right thing."

Christopher Columbus, a Christian, kept a journal while sailing to the New World. Although there were some exciting events during his trip and even times of real drama, the most common entry in his journal was, "Today we sailed on." Some days in life—most days—are like that; often we just have to keep going. Our patient endurance will be rewarded over the long haul, though. Hebrews 12 tells us to "run with perseverance the race marked out

God works in us for a very (sometimes it seems more like very, very, v-e-r-y) long time. We generally don't see the results immediately.

for us." It talks about Jesus, who "endured the cross." We are exhorted, "Consider him who endured such opposition from sinful men, so that you will not grow weary and lose heart" (Hebrews 12:1–3).

We recently put an addition onto our house. In the process we were forced to cut down a couple of really big oak trees in our back yard. After the trees were down, one of my sons tried counting the growth rings in the trees. On one tree he counted more than one hundred rings. Those trees were huge and deeply rooted. They could not have been easily knocked over. It took the bull-dozer operator three hours to remove one of the stumps. Obviously, though, those trees didn't get that big overnight. It took years of growth to become that solid. Isaiah says that the people of God will be called "trees of righteousness" (Isaiah 61:3). That's exciting, but it's not an overnight process. It takes time. By causing us to wait, God builds His character in us.

Part of the problem in this area is that we do not generally see things from God's perspective. We see steps 1, 2, 3, and 4. God sees 1A, 1B, 1C, etc. When we think we should be at step 4, quite possibly we are really only at 1D because of numerous steps that we never really considered.

> When Lord Clive, as a young man, in the spirit of adventure set out from his British home for India, the ship upon which he sailed was caught in a terrible storm. Continuous adverse gales drove it far off the course, until it finally limped into a South American harbor. There he had to remain for many months before being able to get passage to India.
>
> But during the long wait he acquired the Portuguese language. This qualified him when he did reach India to take an important position with the East India Company, ultimately resulting in his being appointed by the crown as Governor General of India.[2]

It should be noted that we do not always recognize the growth that is taking place in our lives. Sometimes it is so slow that we miss what is happening. However, Scripture promises, "And as the Spirit of the Lord works within us, we become more and more like him" (2 Corinthians 3:18b, TLB).

There is a mall where my wife and I have shopped many times. It is a large, sprawling complex with corridors angled in different directions. Recently they have been doing some major renovations on the mall, and one section currently has no stores. You can still walk down the hallway to other stores, but on either side of the hallway plywood panels separate the construction zone from the general public. Although I've never seen it, behind those panels there is surely a bustle of activity. There are workers constructing walls, installing plumbing and electrical apparatus, and putting in floor coverings and windows. The work has been going on for a long time. However, once the behind-the-scenes work is complete, the panels will come down and people will think, "Wow! Last week there were plywood panels, and now look. Didn't that go quickly?" Because they never saw the actual work, many will be surprised at the result.

God's work in us is often quite similar. It is rarely a fast process. He works in us for a very (sometimes it seems more like very, very, v-e-r-y) long time. We generally don't see the results immediately. However, it is often fascinating how someone who has not seen us for a long time will notice a difference that we have overlooked. God will indeed use those long periods of waiting—causing us to be patient—to build His character in us.

$\mathcal{T}$ESTING CHARACTER

B efore my final closing comments, one other concept is important to mention here. God often uses the tough times of life to *build* character in us. However, He will often *test* that character through the easy times. Paul told us that he had learned to be satisfied in all situations. "I have learned to be content whatever the circumstances. I know what it is to be in need, and I know what it is to have plenty. I have learned the secret of being content in any and every situation, whether well fed or hungry, whether living in plenty or in want" (Philippians 4:11–12). Our natural way of thinking is that the real test is being content when we are in want. When we are well fed, when we have plenty, what is the test in that? It's easy to be content when everything is going your way.

> *God often uses the tough times of life to* build *character in us. However, He will often* test *that* character *through the easy times.*

On the surface this seems true. However, we must understand that real contentedness does not come from having everything. It comes from being in relationship with God. In fact, having everything we desire often leads to complacency, not contentedness. It becomes easy to have the attitude, "I've got everything I want. I don't need God."

It is during the times when life appears to be going great that God allows us to see how much character has been developed in us. When our ship comes in, it is all too easy for us to become cocky and self-satisfied. We can begin to think like King Nebuchadnezzar in the Old Testament. One day in the midst of his great triumphs and amazing prosperity, he said, "Is not this the great Babylon I have built as the royal residence, by my mighty power and for the glory of my majesty?" (Daniel 4:30). This is the same king who had seen so much godly character in the lives of Daniel,

Shadrach, Meshach, and Abednego that he put them in charge of much of his kingdom. He saw the mighty hand of God rescue Shadrach, Meshach, and Abednego from the fiery furnace and acknowledged that their God had done it. Later he mentioned, "I, Nebuchadnezzar, was at home in my palace, contented and prosperous" (Daniel 4:4), and then went on to tell of the dream he had, warning him not to be so haughty with what had been given to him as the king. Unfortunately none of this seemed to have any long-term effects on the king. When the time of testing came—the moment of having everything he wanted—he failed the test.

> Twelve months later, as the king was walking on the roof of the royal palace of Babylon, he said, "Is not this the great Babylon I have built as the royal residence, by my mighty power and for the glory of my majesty?"
>
> The words were still on his lips when a voice came from heaven, "This is what is decreed for you, King Nebuchadnezzar: Your royal authority has been taken from you. You will be driven away from people and will live with the wild animals; you will eat grass like cattle. Seven times will pass by for you until you acknowledge that the Most High is sovereign over the kingdoms of men and gives them to anyone He wishes."
>
> Immediately what had been said about Nebuchadnezzar was fulfilled. He was driven away from people and ate grass like cattle. His body was drenched with the dew of heaven until his hair grew like the feathers of an eagle and his nails like the claws of a bird (Daniel 4:29–33).

When we are prosperous it is easy for us think more highly of ourselves than we should. Because of this we can be unwilling to show kindness to those less fortunate. It can be difficult to be humble when you are living a life of ease. How often each of us has seen the person whose life is suddenly on easy street become haughty and arrogant and treat others in less than gentle ways.

> *Someone once said, "If I had known there was going to be a test, I would have studied for it." Unfortunately, nearly all of God's tests are pop quizzes.*

Times of seemingly great triumph can be similar tests. In my life God has used many things to show me my heart. For example, there have been times when people have told me what a profound impact my writing or teaching has had on them. When I do something for which I am recognized, it is increasingly important for me to remember Who gave me the abilities to do those things. This was not simply a personal victory. God's hand must be recognized in it, and I must see Him as the real victor. If not, I can become smug and think, *Look at what I have accomplished.* Solomon said, "The crucible for silver and the furnace for gold, but man is tested by the praise he receives" (Proverbs 27:21). When I begin to think that I have accomplished something on my own, I just failed the test. There is no humility being displayed there—only pride and self-sufficiency.

Someone once said, "If I had known there was going to be a test, I would have studied for it." Unfortunately, nearly all of God's tests are pop quizzes. There is no prior notice given. They can come about at any time and at any place. That is why we must allow God to build His character in us—not just a pretty veneer on the outside but something that permeates our being and becomes part and parcel of who we are. When character qualities like kindness and gentleness, honesty and diligence have been driven deeply inside us through the trials of life, then and only then are we able to pass tests like ease of life, prosperity, and admiration.

EPILOGUE

We have spent a lot of time discussing specific character qualities and how they become reality in our lives. At this point it should be stressed that possessing all of the character qualities we have discussed in this book will not make you more acceptable to God. Even having each of them in large measure will not cause the Lord to love you more than He already does. Too often we have a tendency to lean toward self-importance "and pronouncing about our life accomplishments as if they were things we could pile on a little red wagon and trundle in to God to solicit His approval and add to our pride of achievement."[1] It doesn't work. God does not care about us because we are nice folks. Even if we personify to the fullest measure all of the character qualities mentioned in this book (as well as others not mentioned), that will not cause the Lord to love us more than He already does. God loves you. Period. His mercy and grace are extended to you every moment of every day.

Understanding this foundational truth, it is also clear from Scripture that God wants us to display character qualities like integrity, gentleness, kindness, and humility. He wants us to live what we know. He wants our lives to match what we say we believe. He wants us to act more like Christ every day. He wants to build His character in us.

God has many ways of working His character in us as we submit to Him. Consider for a moment the lives of David and Solomon. Although David certainly made his share of mistakes and wrong choices, the Bible refers to him as a man after God's own heart (Acts 13:22). The psalmist, speaking about the nation of Israel, said: "And David shepherded them with integrity of heart" (Psalm 78:72).

It is obvious that David had a large measure of godly character. When Saul was chasing him, David twice had the opportunity to take revenge and end the life and reign of this man who had become his nemesis. He knew that he, David, would be the next king. It was the perfect opportunity. But David also knew it was the wrong thing to do and therefore refused to do it. His handling of so many situations after he became king revealed the depth of character that God had worked in him. But how did this come about? Where did he acquire this godly character?

David was not born into a wealthy family. His family had to work to make their living. David's job in the family was apparently the least pleasant. Actually, it was one of the most despised jobs in that society—tending sheep. He quite probably spent years with those sheep. Oh, certainly it was not a continuous twenty-four-hour a day, seven-day per week slavery position. However, it seems fairly safe to assume that he at least occasionally spent entire days and even nights with the sheep. On more than one occasion he had to defend his flock against vicious wild animals. This was not a nine-to-five, pencil-pushing desk job. He worked, and he worked hard. There were undoubtedly lonely, bitterly cold, scary nights; hot, parched, sun-scorched days; unknown predators; long periods of boredom; etc. All of this was prior to the more intense period of his life when he would fight in battles and run for his life from mad king Saul. Though perhaps this is not our picture of the ideal life, it was a perfect scenario for building character: patience, endurance, perseverance, suffering, time to pray and worship—all the necessary elements were there.

During this time of testing and character building, the psalms David wrote suggest that he had learned the spiritual disciplines that help build character in us. Although he did not have the Bible as we know it today, he obviously knew the history of his people and regularly recalled God's faithfulness to his forefathers. Many of David's songs are a model of honest prayer to God. David also clearly understood worship. Additionally, his relationship with Jonathan is often used even today as a model of serious accountability, and David unquestionably yielded himself to the Lord again and again.

David's son Solomon, however, had a life of ease. He was born into the household of the man who quite probably had become the richest, most powerful man on earth at the time. With regard to material possessions, Solomon never lacked anything throughout his lifetime. He enjoyed the proverbial born-with-the-silver-spoon-in-his-mouth existence. Solomon had it made, but he lacked character. Toward the end of his days he was a bitter, jaded man living a grossly sinful life. He never had to go through the character-building steps that his father, David, went through. Because of that, character was lacking. When Solomon's life was tested in good times, unfortunately he failed the test.

God desires to build His character in your life and mine. Although we may not always recognize His hand, God is indeed at work in our lives. There have been times in my life when I wondered if all this effort on God's part was really having an effect. Let me assure you that it is.

Most people—myself included—have a few half-finished projects sitting around the house. When we get a little extra time, we are confident that those things will get finished. God's Word promises us, "He who began a good work in you will carry it on to completion until the day of Christ Jesus" (Philippians 1:6). God will not leave us half-finished. He will complete the work He began.

In his book *The Call*, Os Guiness put it this way:

> Perhaps you are frustrated by the gap that still remains between your vision and your accomplishments. Or you may be depressed by the pages

of your life that are blotched with compromises, failures, betrayals, and sin. You have had your say. Others may have had their say. But make no judgments and draw no conclusions until the scaffolding of history is stripped away and you see what it means for God to have had His say—and made you what you are called to be.[2]

God is not finished with you. He is at work in your life on a daily basis. Allow Him to have His full sway in your life as He builds the kind of character in you that He desires.

As you move on from reading this book, you may need to refer back to it—maybe even on a regular basis. Remember, the strength to change, even the desire to change, comes from Him. Set your standards high to live what you already know. When you miss the mark, yield to the conviction of the Holy Spirit and repent. Do your part to abide in Him and His Word, which will always change you. Submit patiently to the trials that test and develop your character. Know that "He who began a good work in you will carry it on to completion."

Notes

Chapter 1: Becoming More Like Jesus

1. John Ortberg, *The Life You've Always Wanted*. Grand Rapids, Michigan: Zondervan Publishing House, 1997.

Chapter 2: Character—What's Inside

1. James Emery White, *You Can Experience a Purposeful Life*. Waco, Texas: Word Books.

2. C.S. Lewis, *Mere Christianity*. New York, New York: Macmillan Publishing Co., Inc., 1943, 1945, 1952.

3. *The Teacher's Commentary*. Scripture Press Publications, 1987.

Chapter 7: The Strength of Gentleness

1. Gary L. Thomas, "The Genius of Gentleness," *Christian Reader*, May/June, 1999. Condensed from *Discipleship Journal* (Issue One Hundred Eight, 1998), © 1998 Gary L. Thomas. Used by permission. Originally adapted from *The Glorious Pursuit* (NavPress), © 1998 Gary L. Thomas.

Chapter 9: The Duty of Diligence

1. *DAWN Report* (Issue No. 26, February 1996), Colorado Springs, Colorado: DAWN Ministries.

Chapter 11: The Lost Art of Loyalty

1. *The Pastor's Weekly Briefing* (Vol. 6, No. 14, April 3, 1998), Colorado Springs, Colorado: Focus on the Family.

Chapter 12: The Freedom of Self-Control

1. *The Teacher's Commentary*. Scripture Press Publications, 1987.

2. C.S. Lewis, *Mere Christianity*. New York, New York: Macmillan Publishing Co., Inc., 1943, 1945, 1952.

Chapter 13: The Trick of Taming the Tongue

1. Elise Arndt, *A Mother's Touch*. Wheaton, Illinois: SP Publications/Victor Books, 1983.

2. Bill Myers, *The Portal*. Minneapolis, Minnesota: Bethany House Publishers, 1991.

Chapter 14: The Goal of Gratefulness

1. Quoted by Os Guinness, *The Call*. Nashville, Tennessee: Word Publishing, 1998.

Chapter 17: The Importance of Excellence

1. Os Guinness, *The Call*. Nashville, Tennessee: Word Publishing, 1998.

2. Ibid.

Chapter 18: It Is God's Work

1. Philip Yancey, *The Jesus I Never Knew*. Grand Rapids, Michigan: Zondervan Publishing House, 1995.

2. John Piper, *A Godward Life*. Sisters, Oregon: Multnomah Publishers Inc., 1997.

3. Steve Fry, *I Am*. Sisters, Oregon: Multnomah Publishers Inc., 2000.

4. John Ortberg, *The Life You've Always Wanted*. Grand Rapids, Michigan: Zondervan Publishing House, 1997.

Chapter 19: Grace Makes All the Difference

1. Horatius Bonar, *God's Way of Holiness*. Durham, England: Evangelical Press, 1979; originally published 1864.

2. Jerry Bridges, *The Discipline of Grace*. Colorado Springs, Colorado: NavPress, 1994.

Chapter 20: Gratitude Is Not Enough

1. John Piper, *A Godward Life*. Sisters, Oregon: Multnomah Publishers Inc., 1997.

Chapter 21: Do We Just Wait for God to Zap Us with Godly Character?

1. C.S. Lewis, *Mere Christianity*. New York, New York: Macmillan Publishing Co., Inc., 1943, 1945, 1952.

2. Hannah Whithall Smith, *The Christian's Secret of a Happy Life*. Uhrichsville, Ohio: Barbour Publishing, Inc., 1998.

3. Jerry Bridges, *The Discipline of Grace*. Colorado Springs, Colorado: NavPress, 1994.

4. Richard, J. Foster, *Celebration of Discipline*. New York, New York: Harper and Row Publishers, 1978.

Chapter 22: Scripture Study and Memorization

1. Jack Hayford, *Living the Spirit-Formed Life*. Ventura, California: Regal/Gospel Light, 2001.

2. *The Teacher's Commentary*. Scripture Press Publications, 1987.

3. Mark Buchanan, *Your God Is Too Safe*. Sisters, Oregon: Multnomah Publishers Inc., 2001.

Chapter 23: Prayer

1. Richard, J. Foster, *Celebration of Discipline*. New York, New York: Harper and Row Publishers, 1978.

2. Jim Cymbala, *Fresh Wind, Fresh Fire*. Grand Rapids, Michigan: Zondervan Publishing House, 1997.

3. Bob Sorge, *In His Face*. Canandaigua, New York: Oasis House, 1994.

4. Donald S. Whitney, *Spiritual Disciplines of the Christian Life*. Colorado Springs, Colorado: Navpress Publishing Group, 1991.

Chapter 25: Making Right Choices

1. Philip Yancey, *Reaching for the Invisible God*. Grand Rapids, Michigan: Zondervan Publishing House, 2000.

Chapter 28: God's Other Method: Adversity

1. Robert Moeller, *Love in Action*. Sisters, Oregon: Multnomah Books, 1994.

2. Bernard Ruffin, *Fanny Crosby—The Hymn Writer*. Uhrichsville, Ohio: Barbour Publishing, 1995.

3. Ibid.

Chapter 29: Patience—The Process

1. Frank Peretti, *The Visitation*. Nashville, Tennessee: Word Publishing, 1999.

2. *Prairie Overcomer*, quoted in *Encyclopedia of 7700 Illustrations*, Paul Lee Tan. Chicago, Illinois: R.R. Donnelley and Sons, Inc., 1979.

Epilogue

1. Os Guinness, *The Call*. Nashville, Tennessee: Word Publishing, 1998.

2. Ibid.

ORDER THESE OTHER GREAT BOOKS BY TOM KRAEUTER

Living Beyond the Ordinary $10.00 Eternal life starts now. Are you 100% satisfied with your Christian life? If not, then maybe it's time to start living beyond the ordinary! Practical steps to an extraordinary relationship with God.

If Standing Together Is So Great, Why Do We Keep Falling Apart? $9.00 The church in America is missing much of the power of God because of a lack of unity. You'll learn why unity is so vital as well as specific steps of how to make it reality.

Worship Is...What?! $9.00 In his usual story-filled way, Tom makes the scriptures come alive for today. If you want to understand what worship is all about—or if you think you already do—you should read this book.

Keys to Becoming an Effective Worship Leader $9.00 An in-depth look at what it really means to be a worship leader. These insights have proven helpful to worship leaders worldwide.

Developing an Effective Worship Ministry $9.00 The A-Z book on developing the ministry of praise and worship in the local church.

The Worship Leader's Handbook $9.00 Question and answer format makes this a great reference book.

These are some of the most practical books available for worship leaders. They will inspire you and give you a solid foundation for the ministry of praise and worship.

Things They Didn't Teach Me in Worship Leading School $10.00 50 prominent worship leaders from around the world share stories.

More Things They Didn't Teach Me in Worship Leading School $10.00 Sequel to the popular *Things They Didn't Teach Me...*

To order write to:
Training Resources
8929 Old LeMay Ferry Rd.
Hillsboro MO 63050

Or call:
888-333-1724
M-F, 9:00-4:00 CST
(charge card orders only)

Or visit our web site:
www.training-resources.org